CONTENTS

FOREWORD

It should be, I think, the purpose of any book about forgotten giants and heroes to not only place them in their time and to catalog their accomplishments but, in some way, to orient them into the peculiarities of the special cultural patterns of their moment.

These men, these five, half-remembered, occasionally honored, have now become, each in a separate way, an acknowledged source, a kind of headwater that made possible major contributions to the art or the science of architecture. None of them are far enough in the past to have completely acquired the easy acceptance of the historical footnote. Three of them lived close enough to the present and, although half-forgotten but for particularly interested specialists, made occasional forays into the contemporary scene.

Of those who knew them intimately or through painstaking studies unearthed their beginnings, Esther McCoy has brought to this book a careful and perceptive judgment, a loving recognition, and a sound critical eye.

These were men with a kind of stubborn courage, who, battling with their own convictions, managed somehow to overcome a host of obstacles; in many cases, it would seem, by sheer strength of will and purpose. They built without compromise and too often without reward, proceeding sometimes slowly, sometimes with what seemed amazing intuition. Each in his very separate way worked through a deep knowledge of the present and future, arriving at brilliant solutions to the problems at hand, often transcending architecture and marking himself as an innovator. These were by no means men who did merely handsome or arresting things. They were men who made basic contributions to structure. They developed, with the almost primitive facilities available to them, systems and techniques which were only to be fully realized in a later time, in a wider industrialization of the building field. These men loved the materials with which they worked, and invented and devised means of putting them together not only from the past experience of their profession but with an almost intuitive esthetic in giving the work a form, and a pre-

science that created bold outlines for the future development of the human environment.

While it is true their architecture did not limit itself to any particular style, unless it could be called peculiarly their own, they did create an attitude, a kind of creative climate that has maintained a strong and easily recognizable line of consistency to the present.

It would be impossible to understand the admittedly great influence of western American architecture without an appreciative knowledge of their work. Having gone through periods of creative excitement and of admiring imitativeness, the least that can be said of this architecture is that it has always exhibited an enormous curiosity, vitality, and a willingness to experiment resulting, for better or for worse, in a body of work that stands up to the controversy in which it always seems to be involved.

Many of us, from time to time, have attempted to understand and to explain the remarkable conditions that have made possible the variety and the solid accomplishments that have occurred here. Perhaps, among other things, it was easier to break from a tradition that had its roots so far away, and thereby escape the social and professional consequences of disapproval that comes from doing the same things, over and over again.

While most of the credit must, of course, go to those professionals involved whose creative curiosity led them into, if not unknown, at least untried fields, something should be said for the clients who were willing to take part in the adventure and to risk considerably more than the substance of their dreams. These are the comparatively unknown but often wonderfully rewarded participants.

It is too obviously true that the generative seed never really exists unless there is fertile ground to receive it. At least, it does seem that in this particular area, there was a collusion of circumstances, of nature and of a kind of people who, confronted with possibility of a new kind of life, created an idiom that best expressed an untried pattern of living. There continues to be an enormously generative impulse and an amalgam of cultural patterns in conflict and in constant readjustment that outlines a highly special point of view which still irritates and delights many of those who observe it.

The architect, as a disciplined professional, has had to create within a framework of limitations, to contend with, and often to write, the rules by which he works. In their day he had to be not only a practitioner, but also a teacher, and it was his responsibility to excite and enliven shoals of younger men whose work later assumed a commanding position in the profession. The results have been a happy renewal of all the early promise, and it is to be hoped that all this will continue to confound and reward us.

None of us, I am sure, has any idea of what will happen in the immediate future. However, with what we know of the men presently at work, and of these men who preceded them, there is reason to believe that the enormous fertility of western American architecture will continue to enrich, infuriate and enliven both the professional and nonprofessional world of building. This creative continuity is certainly not to be accomplished without wide differences of opinion, but it is doubtful that any other American region in our time has so quickly developed such an invigorating architectural idiom.

JOHN ENTENZA
Editor, *Arts & Architecture*

INTRODUCTION

This edition of *Five California Architects* is printed from the original plates, with the advantage of preserving Paul Grotz's handsome design but with the disadvantage of perpetuating certain errors in the text. We were writing in 1956–58 on little-explored subjects in which interest was then limited. No one seemed to be watching except W. W. Atkin, the publisher. The advance went toward assembling what still seems to be an excellent collection of new and archive photographs, plans, details, and sketches.

My text was trimmed by the publisher, which left two holes. The belief of some historians that

Irving Gill's style was influenced by Viennese newspaper articles by Adolf Loos (1897–1900) may have been caused by a deletion. Gill had asked his nephew to study German so that the latter could translate for him. Louis Gill's later assertion that he did not was cut from the text. (The Reverend John Gill, son of Louis, chairman of the examining chaplains of the Los Angeles Diocese: "I never heard my father indicate in any way that he knew German." Lloyd Wright, a Gill draftsman: "No one in the office knew German.") Furthermore, I find no evidence of publication of Loos's work, except a few interiors, before 1904, when Gill's style began to crystallize. However, both men may have heeded Louis Sullivan's article "Ornament in Architecture": Gill was a draftsman in the Adler and Sullivan office in 1892, when it was published; Loos may have read it in Dresden, where he was a student at the College of Technology (he finished in 1893, the year Gill started practice in San Diego).

Schindler's given names were also deleted. They are Rudolph Michael: He disliked the first, was called by the second, and for thirty-two years practiced architecture as R. M. In the office we called him R. M.

Errata:

Neutra's Lovell house was designed in 1928, completed in 1929. Gill's 1911 Christian Science Church did not replace the one he designed in 1904.

On the Greene and Greene chapter by Randell Makinson: For Judson studios, substitute Lange; the Culbertson house bay window was added in 1914; the date of the Ford house is 1907, the Crow house 1909, the Tichenor house 1904, and the James house 1918; somehow "electrically" came out "electronically" on page 135. These and minor slips are corrected in the Makinson book *Greene and Greene*, to be published by Peregrine Smith in 1975.

ESTHER MCCOY

Santa Monica, California
January, 1975

FIVE CALIFORNIA ARCHITECTS

BERNARD MAYBECK

IRVING GILL

CHARLES and HENRY GREENE

R. M. SCHINDLER

FIVE CALIFORNIA ARCHITECTS

ESTHER McCOY

Chapter on Greene and Greene
by Randell L. Makinson

Praeger Publishers
NEW YORK

Acknowledgments:

First of all, my appreciation goes to Randell L. Makinson for contributing his fine chapter on Greene and Greene. In 1956 Mr. Makinson received his Bachelor of Architecture degree from the University of Southern California, and at the same time was awarded a Rehmann Scholarship by the American Institute of Architects to study the work of the Greenes. While devoting himself to this research, he serves as an instructor in the School of Architecture of USC and also finds time to carry on a practice as a designer.

To John Entenza, publisher and editor of *Arts & Architecture* magazine, which published some of my early writings on the Greenes, Gill and Schindler, from which this book grew.

To James H. Elliott, assistant chief curator of art at the Los Angeles County Museum, who arranged the Gill exhibition in 1958 and commissioned the catalogue, an expanded version of which appears in this book. Marvin Rand's sensitive photography of Gill's work, which appears here, was done for the exhibition.

To James Toland, editor of *Los Angeles Times Home Magazine,* which published many of my articles on Maybeck, Gill, Schindler and the Greenes.

To Lloyd Henry Wright, a pioneer of western architecture, whose devotion to Irving Gill contributed to my understanding of the man and his work; to Louis J. Gill, FAIA, who gave innumerable hours to talks with me about his uncle; to John August Reed, AIA, whose knowledge and appreciation of Gill first led me to attempt research on the subject; to Frederick Gutheim for his information concerning Gill's later years; to Eloise Roorbach for recollections of Gill.

To William H. Jordy, for the loan of photographs of Gill's work in the East.

To William Gray Purcell, AIA, for recalling so cheerfully his memories of Maybeck and Berkeley; to Jack Hillmer for reading the Maybeck chapter and for his encouragement; to Kelly Buchanan, William C. Hays, FAIA, Gerard Hurley, and Florence Dickens Gray for aid in the Maybeck research.

To Richard J. Neutra, FAIA, for his recollections of Schindler's student days in Vienna; to Franziska Schindler Bojczuk for notes on her brother; to Pauline G. Schindler and Edith Gutterson for information about Schindler's days in Chicago and Taliesin; to C. Vick Santocchi, AIA, for suggestions on the Schindler chapter.

To L. Morgan Yost, FAIA, whose researches in the early forties on the Greenes and Maybeck opened up again an almost forgotten chapter of American architecture.

To Margaret Nixon and Helen Caton for editorial assistance.

To my husband, whose good spirits sustained me during the year the book was in the typewriter.

PUBLISHED IN THE UNITED STATES OF AMERICA IN 1975
BY PRAEGER PUBLISHERS, INC.
111 FOURTH AVENUE, NEW YORK, N.Y. 10003

© 1960 BY ESTHER MC COY
INTRODUCTION © 1975 BY PRAEGER PUBLISHERS, INC.

DESIGN BY PAUL GROTZ

ORIGINALLY PUBLISHED IN 1960 BY REINHOLD BOOK CORPORATION

LIBRARY OF CONGRESS CATALOG CARD NUMBER 74-19818

ISBN 0-275-46690-6 (CLOTH)
ISBN 0-275-71720-8 (PAPER)

PRINTED IN THE UNITED STATES OF AMERICA

BERNARD MAYBECK

1862-1957

In the 1880's when *avant garde* architects in Chicago were calling for freedom from the past and championing the new and revolutionary steel skeleton, Bernard Ralph Maybeck was a student at the Parisian stronghold of academic tradition, L'École des Beaux Arts. Completely absorbed by the classic wonders of Greece and by the Romanesque and early Gothic churches of the Middle Ages, he was unaffected by the surrounding examples of the Iron Age and unaware of the current architectural revolt against traditionalism.

He studied in the atelier of M. Jules Louis André, who, two decades earlier, had influenced another American student, Henry Hobson Richardson. Although many changes had taken place, Père André was still teaching the idea of beauty and introducing his students to the "influences of the big minds surrounding them" in the architecture of the city.

Maybeck's first assignment there was crucial in forming his fundamental approach to architecture. It was a sketch of a bust and a pedestal,

Detail of entrance, Christian Science Church, Berkeley, 1910.

1

and he drew it in as little time as it had taken him to stretch the paper on his board. When he had finished, Père André said, "Now study it." Maybeck looked at his sketch but found nothing to study either in the bust or the two parallelograms that formed the pedestal.

Then Père André began with his black pencils and marked until the beautiful Whatman paper was almost black. He was hunting for lines that would harmonize with the bust. "You think the thickness of a line doesn't matter?" he asked. "Very well, put that thickness at the end of your nose and see!"

This lesson made a lasting impression on Maybeck, and from then on architecture for him was the study of lines. All his life he made his preliminary sketches without T-square or triangles. He drew them with charcoal, with his fingers, and with an eraser through the black dust on the paper. He made innumerable changes, then darkened the lines he liked best. He also made a tracing which he studied as if it were a classic column, and often made slides and projected them onto a wall for further study. Only when he was sure he had what he wanted did he work for his dimensions.

"I have never been an architect, I just like one line better than another," he said late in his career.*

Maybeck was short in stature, genial in nature, and possessed a decided flair for drama. He dramatized everything, from the smallest incident to his largest building. He had a peasant sturdiness which set him apart from the other American students at the Beaux Arts who had come from backgrounds of wealth or culture. It was quite by chance that he was studying among this elite group at all.

His father, a woodcarver by trade, had emigrated to the United States from Germany in 1848, and Bernard was born on February 7, 1862 in New York City. His mother decided that her first son must become an artist, and although she died before Bernard was three, his father was determined to carry out her wishes.

"Other boys played ball. I had to draw and draw," Maybeck said of his childhood. While attending public school, he was also enrolled in

* Unless otherwise credited, all statements attributed to Maybeck are from taped interviews in the library of Radio Station KPFA, Berkeley, California, or from conversations between the author and Mr. Maybeck.

two private ones, where at an early age he studied French, German, and philosophy. However, his mind was usually somewhere else than on his books. He was busy designing an airplane when he should have been studying chemistry. His father, an agnostic, introduced him to "such important people and events" as Robespierre and the French Revolution, but for all his extra-curricular education he failed in several subjects. Since it was clear that Bernard was not cut out to be a scholar, he was apprenticed, at the age of seventeen, to a wood carver, at $3.00 a month to learn his father's craft. The job was short-lived, for Bernard could not be depended upon to carry out his employer's orders. "I knew what I was doing but he didn't," Bernard said. He then went to work for his father who was in charge of fifty woodcarvers in a shop on lower Broadway where fine furniture was made. Perhaps in despair because his son was too free in injecting his own ideas into a design he was copying, perhaps to carry out his wife's wishes, Maybeck's father made up his mind to send Bernard off to Paris to study furniture designing. In that field the boy's independence might be an asset. So at eighteen, smoking his first cigar, a present from his father's employer, Bernard "reeled onto the boat for France."

The shop where Bernard was apprenticed in Paris was across the street from the Beaux Arts, and one day he saw something that caught his fancy—"a wonderful individual who was wearing a pot hat and kid gloves. He was an architect." Maybeck wrote to his father at once and asked for permission to study at the Beaux Arts.

However, the pot hat was only a clinching argument, for Maybeck's interest in architecture had already begun to develop. He had discovered a shortcut to his favorite lunchtime restaurant through the old Romanesque church of St. Germain des Prés. The church made no particular impression on him until the day he heard singing and sat down to listen. After that he sat there for a little while every day and gradually began to feel an emotional quality in the church itself.

He experienced the same feeling later on in the Romanesque churches in the south of France, Ste. Madeleine's in Vezelay, in the Le Puy Cathedral in Auvergne. As he explained it, "The Romanesque period had a trust in some-

thing, something it was confident existed. There was a sincerity in regard to religion that lasted up through the early Gothic to the middle of the thirteenth century. With the Renaissance and the Industrial Revolution they forgot about architecture. The first fifty cathedrals were sort of signposts of the hearts of the French people."

As the walls lightened and the windows and "excrescences on the top" increased in number and size, the interest was in detail rather than masses. He felt that with this plastic development came worldliness. Even the twelfth century Notre Dame was a little too worldly for Maybeck, but he liked the way the towers were cut off "clean and easy. But Rheims? If you want to say that filagree is beautiful, all right."

Unself-consciously he projected himself into the role of builder of other ages: "When you think of things of the past they come alive again." Because of his gift for finding the spirit of the people of each period, architecture had a freshness and an immediacy. For him there was no dead architecture. All ages were the present, and when he became a practicing architect he went to the past to be refreshed, as he dipped into the industrial world of the twentieth century, bringing together disparate elements in a timeless world of his own dramatic creation.

Unclaimed for years by the moderns or the men of the Beaux Arts system, no one was more surprised than Maybeck when in the thirties and forties he was declared to be a pioneer of the modern movement.

The Berkeley architect, Walter R. Ratcliffe, called him "A barbarian among the strictly Renaissance men." Although Maybeck's love for the Ecole never wavered, the system was too cramped for so joyous and independent a spirit. He ranged over the architectural styles freely, picking and choosing forms and motifs. He had no fondness for the axial symmetry of the Renaissance, for the appropriate plan meant too much to him—plan was "the backbone of anything beautiful."

To the inflexible Beaux Arts men who were laced into the system Maybeck was a buffoon. He was unable to do a simple copy of some *hotel de ville*. No style was fixed or sacred to him.

As a modern architect he was an eclectic. The Columbian Exposition of 1893 in Chicago, which opened the door to the classic revival, had for him "the deep idea of beauty." What modern architecture he saw, he thought was ugly. In San Francisco he preferred some monumental derivative work to Willis Polk's 1918 glass-curtain Hallidie Building. He never saw a work of Sullivan's in his life. "But that draftsman of his—what's his name? Frank Lloyd Wright. He's a marvel. We're both Greeks, Wright and I."

He was a mystic, and his architecture was pervaded by mysticism. But above all he wanted to be understood—"When you are talking about something tell the people what you are talking about." He designed for "the man in the street. He's the person you have to please, for he's the one who'll buy the building after the owner sells it." He believed that all worthy creations in architecture sprang from the fraternity between the artist and the workman, as in the Middle Ages, and that "it is spoiled when the gentry gets hold of the idea."

"The artist suspects that it is not the object nor the likeness of the object that he is working for, but a particle of life behind the visible. Here he comes face to face with the real things of life; no assistance can be given him; he cannot hire a boy in gold buttons to open the door to the Muse, nor a clerk nor an accountant to do the drudgery. He is alone with his problem and drifts away from superficial portrayals. After this he strives to find the spiritual meaning of things and to transmit the secret to the lay-man." (From Maybeck's booklet, *The Palace of Fine Arts and Lagoon,* Paul Elder, 1915.)

The secrets Maybeck transmitted embodied all the principles of the new architecture. His plans broke with precedent to create a background for what we now consider modern living. He was ingenious in solving the problems of bringing light into his buildings. He linked living areas to gardens. He used materials directly and with craftsmanship, while taking full advantage of technology. He created new and personal forms that arose naturally out of plan. He was inventive, and his solutions were so correct that they have become a part of the common architectural fund.

Maybeck's career in architecture started in 1886 after he had passed his examinations at the Beaux Arts and returned home. A former roommate at school, Thomas Hastings, had just opened an office, and the new firm of Carrère and Hastings was designing the Ponce de Leon

Hotel in St. Petersburg, Florida. They gave Maybeck his first job. He and Hastings were both twenty-five years old.

Hastings, with Maybeck at his elbow did most of preliminary planning of the enormous Spanish Renaissance hotel. They studied the lines of the building as they had studied their drawings at school. But now school was out. The hotel was more Mexican than Spanish and like the Mexicans, who put their own personal stamp on each successive style exported from Spain, the young men strayed from their subject. The carved arch of the entrance and the plane surfaces might have come out of a Mexican Romanesque building, while the organization of the windows was similar to work of Richardson and Wright.

When construction was started Maybeck was sent to Florida to superintend the work. His father went with him to execute some of the wood carvings. Bernard's presence on the job accounted for some of the exuberance of the interiors. Carrère and Hastings were "never again to design anything as rash as this hotel; to be coolly competent, that was their highest aim, and if they did better than they intended, it was because they were artists in spite of themselves," Wayne Andrews wrote in his book *Architecture, Ambition and Americans* (Harper, 1955).

In 1958 the hotel was chosen by the American Institute of Architects for its "One Hundred Years of American Architecture" exhibition.

After the hotel was finished in 1888, Maybeck joined forces with another former classmate, James Russell, and together they set up practice in Kansas City, Russell's home town. However, they were unable to secure any commissions and their partnership was brief. In Kansas City, Maybeck met a school teacher, Mark White, and his sister Annie. In 1889 White and Maybeck set out for San Francisco, and the following year Maybeck and Annie White were married.

Maybeck was profoundly influenced by the indigenous building he found in the Bay Area— the simple shingled houses weathered to a warm lovely brown. In Berkeley where the Maybecks lived, these houses were often half-hidden among the trees.

Maybeck worked for a brief time in the office of Ernest Coxhead, an Englishman, who also had a sympathetic feeling for the craftsmanlike

shingled builders' house and successfully crossed it with the Queen Anne cottage. He used redwood boards in large dimensions, which especially appealed to Maybeck. Although Coxhead designed very few houses, he brought some of the sound principles of William Morris into play.

Less is known of Maybeck's domestic architecture than of his other work, but it was a field in which he excelled. Many of his practices came from the indigenous house, whose virtues of plan, orientation, temperature control, and direct use of materials were later to influence a whole California school of architecture.

For a while Maybeck worked for a furniture manufacturer designing and carving furniture. Then, when the Crocker Building in San Francisco was being designed in 1891, the architect, A. Page Brown, hired Maybeck as a draftsman. One of Maybeck's details became his colophon— the entwined initials A and M for Annie Maybeck, which appeared in the terra cotta decoration on the building. In the Swedenborgian Church, commissioned to Brown in 1894, Maybeck's hand was clearer, but there was no prediction of the mystical atmosphere he was to achieve in the Christian Science Church or the simple shingled Unitarian Church for Palo Alto.

In 1894 Maybeck accepted a teaching post at the University of California in the Department of Drawing; he taught descriptive geometry, a subject in which he had received a silver medal at the Beaux Arts. The offer was made, however, because there was no one else available who knew the subject. He was soon teaching a class in architecture, which met informally at his home. Out of this beginning grew the university's College of Architecture as well as the Phoebe Apperson Hearst competition for a university master plan.

William C. Hays, who was one of the early members of the department, and Kenneth Cardwell, Assistant Professor of Architecture, told of Maybeck's meeting with Mrs. Hearst.

Mrs. Hearst came to the university one day in 1896 to offer funds for a mining building to be built in memory of her husband. "There she was with the money in her hand, and like a good executive, President Kellogg assured her that if she would return in a day or two he would be able to show her what they could do with the money. A hurried call to the engineering department found no talent to produce in twenty-four hours a drawing of an imaginary building. But someone did recall that there was that architect fellow, Maybeck, around and if an architect was good for anything maybe this was it." (From *California Monthly*, April, 1954.)

Mrs. Hearst accepted Maybeck's preliminary plan for the Mining Building, but when it came to placing it on the campus he was convinced that the time had come to think about a master plan. In 1862 Frederick Law Olmsted had planned the 124-acre campus of the university but as in most universities, the placing of buildings had been left to chance.

Maybeck felt that the over-all design should be the work of someone outside the university because, as he wrote in *The Planning of a University*, "the more he is influenced by individuals the more likely he is to lose himself in details, which should come later, and the less likely is the composition to be broad. . . ."

In the 1900 issue of the college annual, *Blue and Gold*, he wrote of the plan, "Even if we err toward the brilliant, which is not probable, time will give to the whole that earnestness and seriousness that will awaken love in the hearts of the men that beheld it."

Nothing could have pleased Mrs. Hearst more than Maybeck's suggestion that an international competition be held for a master plan. The directors of the university saw it in a practical light. Men of wealth would be more willing to endow buildings to perpetuate their names if the buildings were "part of a superb architectural pile that would excite the admiration of the world," as the university historian, William Carey Jones, wrote in 1901.

Thus the Phoebe Apperson Hearst Plan, "the most lavishly endowed architectural competition known to history," was initiated, noted the historian. Overnight the University of California was a topic of discussion in drafting rooms throughout the United States and Europe.

"Not since Aladdin built his famous palace, never since Wren sought and was deprived of the opportunity of rebuilding London according to his own splendid conception, have architects been offered so unique and so transcendent a chance." (From the *London Times* of January 10, 1898.)

Never had a man who loved drama fed on it so richly. As administrator of the plan, May-

beck went first to New York, then to Europe where he was honored in every capital. The program for the competition was drafted at the Beaux Arts which must have made him burst with pride.

"By unrestricted use of the telegraph with Maybeck and Professor Gaudet in Paris, the program was put in final shape," wrote the university historian. Six thousand programs were dispatched, as well as contour maps and photographs of the site and its surroundings.

Mrs. Hearst spent over $100,000 on the competition, enough to construct two buildings, and was toasted in Antwerp by the jury "in the name of the profession and all the sciences." The winning plan now hangs in the foyer of the Campanile on the campus. Because the winner, Emile Bénard, refused to leave his native France, Maybeck, acting for the University Regents, invited John Galen Howard of New York to supervise the execution of the Bénard plan. (Howard had placed fourth with a plan judged to have "general reasonableness.")

The winning plan had been chosen not because it was the best composition, Maybeck said, but because it solved a problem. Bénard's plan could be developed for a future university— "For that he has laid down a principle, and fundamentally you start with the sewer. The sewer is the background to any plan."

Howard took over with a firm hand and Maybeck lost the Mining Building. Work on it was started immediately in Howard's New York office. According to William Gray Purcell, who had worked on the plans for the university buildings as a draftsman in Howard's office, Howard considered Maybeck's work beneath serious consideration. Maybeck's name was greeted with laughter in the drafting room. Soon after Howard moved to California in 1901, he was appointed Professor of Architecture; and Maybeck was suddenly out of a post at the university. In time the Bénard Plan became the Howard Plan.

Maybeck's career at the university was brief and meteoric but no man ever enjoyed so much the events that led to his own overthrow. The only Maybeck buildings on the campus now are the Men's Faculty Club, built before Howard's arrival, and the Hearst Memorial Gymnasium for Women; the gymnasium was designed by Maybeck in association with Julia Morgan, the

First use of the laminated arch was in Hearst Hall, University of California, Berkeley, 1899, shown here under construction. Fifty-four feet from base to apex, it was held together by bracings and straps which could be tightened as required.

The arch was partially enclosed in an outer structure, whose walls were covered with redwood shakes. On top of the outer structure was a roof garden. The building was destroyed by fire in 1922.

architect of San Simeon, in 1927, the year Howard resigned.

During the Hearst competition, however, Maybeck had received several good commissions. In 1899 Mrs. Hearst commissioned him to design "an edifice where she could entertain the university community in general and the women students in particular," wrote Mr. Jones.

Hearst Hall, destroyed by fire in 1922, is still notable in the history of American architecture for the first use of the laminated arch. The form of the building derived from early Gothic style, a period described by Maybeck as "when Gothic was still honest," and when towers were cut off clean and easy. There was, however, as little precedent for Hearst Hall in architecture as there was in engineering.

The university historian described the arches as built up of "moist pine boards lashed together in sufficient thickness, which is greatest where the stress is greatest, and bent to meet the apex." From base to apex the arches were 54 feet high. Around the system of arches, a structure was developed, the exterior walls of which were sheathed with redwood shakes, some natural and some darkened with stain.

The arch form was visible on the exterior only at the ends of the building and near the apex. Two square towers with low-hipped roofs stood on either side of the exposed arch at the entrance. On the sides the straight-walled outer structure stopped two-thirds of the way up; on the roof of the outer structure Maybeck developed promenades. Strollers could look through unglazed openings between each bay down onto the dance floor, or out toward the Berkeley hills and the Bay.

The plan was a rectangle, 60 by 140 feet; the lower floor housed mechanical equipment and a banquet hall seating five hundred. Smoke from heating and cooking was carried underground to the chimney tower. The upper floor was a large open hall, uninterrupted by supports, with a raised stage at one end. The hall was used for dances and college theatricals. Shingles surfaced the interior walls; an example of Maybeck's ornamental effects in wood was the toothed edging above the arches.

The large windows in each bay admitted light; it was a stroke of genius on Maybeck's part to fill in the windows with wooden spindles from Spain. The spindles were strong enough to give structural support and at the same time created a rich pattern. At night when the windows were illuminated from behind by red lights the hall was a place of magic. Hundreds of lights hanging in circular groups from the arches provided full illumination for the interior.

Mrs. Hearst brought some Gobelin tapestries —one came from Barberini Palace—from her collection and hung one in each of the twelve alcoves, and then added a Rembrandt and a Murillo. To divide the dining room into smaller spaces she supplied Egyptian appliqued tapestries, which were hung from structural posts and braces of rough redwood.

After a few years Hearst Hall was cut up into bays and moved onto the campus. According to William Gray Purcell, who witnessed the moving, Maybeck was on the scene, "wearing a tube of a black overcoat, with two tubes of black pant legs flapping against his ankles." (Maybeck designed his own trousers, which reached almost to his armpits.) When one section broke loose and rolled into a ditch, Maybeck and his engineer ran to investigate the extent of the damage. They were relieved to find that the bay wasn't even warped; it was set right and rolled on its way.

Hearst Hall was seen to best advantage when it was turned into a women's gymnasium and the Hearst art was removed. Maybeck designed a pergolaed passage from the building to a basket ball field; the bleachers, also his work, had openings for trees on the site to pass through.

Another laminated arch constructed by Maybeck was for the 1910 San Francisco Settlement Association building. It is used today by a little theatre group. Built up from 1 by 12-inch rough

Mrs. Phoebe Apperson Hearst entertained women students in the main hall, which was also used for dances and college theatricals. Twelve Gobelin tapestries from Mrs. Hearst's collection were hung in the alcoves. Windows above the arches of each bay admitted light through ornamental screens of Spanish spindles, which performed structurally. Red lights, placed between the glass and spindles, cast a rosy glow on the large hall.

Outdoor Art Clubhouse, Mill Valley, 1905. The posts and roof beams extended through the roof and were sheathed in shingles.

The main hall of the clubhouse combined a loving use of wood and sound engineering to achieve uncluttered interior space. The spirit of the building was that of an early English parish church.

King posts of the truss in the Outdoor Art Clubhouse received paired members whose ends were carved with dragon heads.

redwood boards bolted together, this arch was 16 members thick at the point of thrust, and was reduced to four at the base and apex. The declaration of intention was clear in every truss Maybeck designed, but nowhere was it more boastful than in these two laminated arches.

Daring as the laminated arch was, there was no confusion in Maybeck's mind between architecture and engineering. To him, as to Sullivan, "Architecture consists in doing things right. Science consists in inquiring how to do things right." (Letter to *The Craftsman,* December 1908.)

Maybeck's interest in structure did not begin and end with the laminated truss. It followed through his entire work. There was an honesty in his approach to structure that was little understood because of his apparently conflicting interest in decoration. He was not content to follow the modern concept that structure itself was ideal form. More often than not his engineering was hidden by decoration.

However, in a modest two-story French house of 1907, Maybeck cantilevered the floors out from posts that extended up through the second floor and used curtain walls. In the small delightful Outdoor Art Clubhouse in Mill Valley, 1905, he carried his posts and the roof beams outside the main structure and treated them as decorative elements.

Structure to Maybeck was to be lived with, not avoided. He put engineering principles to work for him in the 1906 Hopps house where paired rafters accepted a post between; also in the king post trusses of the Town and Gown Clubhouse, 1899, and the Men's Faculty Club, 1900, as well as the cruciform truss of the 1910 Christian Science Church.

In the 1899 Town and Gown Clubhouse Maybeck followed the best tradition of direct building typical of so many of his early houses. Except for the outrigged cornice structure, the shingled exterior with its candid fenestration was an open book in which the plan within could be read. A system of V-bracing on the lower floor supported the clear space of the hall above. The hall itself, with a handsome open truss and a great fireplace, was like a medieval guild hall or parish church. Time gave a fine patina to the 12- and 14-inch redwood boards which formed a skin for the interior walls. The broad stairway with low risers, repeated by

Town and Gown Clubhouse, Berkeley, 1899. The outrigged cornice structure was typical of Maybeck's spontaneous play with wood.

Men's Faculty Club, University of California, Berkeley, 1900, showed the influence of the missions.

Hopps house, Ross Valley, 1906. May-beck's skill with wood, seen in the branched post, was in the spirit of the "artless art" of the timber countries.

Maybeck in other buildings, created an atmosphere of leisure.

The 1900 Men's Faculty Club, Berkeley, showed the influence of the missions in its arches, low-pitched tile roofs and plaster walls. The outset casement windows cast deep shadows on the walls; and, along with the shingle-covered projection at one end, they broke the expanse of plaster and added dark values which served to bring the mass in closer communication with the ground.

The dining hall was one of Maybeck's most famous interiors. The incongruity of its elements: an open timber roof, round-headed narrow windows, carved dragon heads on the end of the roof purlins, and glass screens created a delightfully tonic atmosphere. In describing his impression of the club's interior, William C. Hays wrote: "Some walls were covered by burlap of citrine color, fastened with narrow wooden strips. The same burlap was used for portieres and for the upholstered seats." (From *Indoors and Out,* May 1906.)

The Faculty Club was one of Maybeck's first experiments with texture in plaster. He disliked the raw newness of plaster and tried to capture the texture of the adobe and straw walls of the missions. In 1900 stucco was considered a cheap imitation of stone, just as shingles were considered proper only for the simple house. Maybeck made them both a part of his vocabulary in architecture.

In his early domestic work Maybeck's explorations were mainly in two directions. The first was the pitched roof, shingled house in the tradition of H. H. Richardson's shingle work of the eighties. A tradition in the spirit of the English crafts movement in the sixties, it brought the vernacular into a closer relationship with official architecture.

The second direction was characterized by more personal forms and by combinations of forms borrowed from historic styles.

During his stay in Europe launching the Hearst Plan, he had picked up many clues to the handling of wood from the village houses of Switzerland and the Scandinavian countries. He did not visit Japan but his imagination served better than a steamship ticket. Some of his houses were like little travelogues. The pagoda roof appeared in his style in 1895 and the chalet in 1900.

→

A light well in the living room of the Tufts house, San Anselmo, 1906, was set flush with the 14-inch redwood wall boards and filtered light through thin slices of mother of pearl shell. It also illuminated two other rooms.

Randolph School, Berkeley, 1910. The 60-degree roof pitch was repeated in the gate structure and the post caps. In the kitchen of the school was a scissor truss, similar to the one seen here.

Interior view of Randolph School, now a private residence. The school represented a new concept in floor planning; classrooms faced terraces on three sides.

→

The light fixture at the entrance stairs in the Tufts house had openings on three sides. Handmade glass was used behind the gold-ornamented wood tracery. The fixture at the right was a second opening for dining room light; the third was in a broom closet in the kitchen.

The 1895 Charles Keeler house, and the studio built a few years later, are examples of these two directions. In the house Maybeck developed a variety of forms and achieved unity in diversity. The various roofs, one a pagoda, had the feeling of a village street whose attached houses had been built by the same carpenter over a period of years.

He exploited this singular approach in the concrete Maurer studio in Berkeley, 1907, and again in the Randolph School, 1910. The latter had three separate 60-degree roofs turned at angles to each other, like a group of three small school houses. The exterior was the result of a fresh approach to plan; each classroom opened on three sides to the garden.

Most of the early domestic work followed the direct forms of the Keeler studio, in which the plan was developed under a simple gable roof. Exterior walls were shingled and wide redwood board and battens formed a continuous skin over the studs, which were sometimes 3 by 4 inches, 24 or 30 inches on center.

Maybeck honored redwood above all materials and used it with love and understanding. Although there was little of his playfulness in the early houses, he achieved simplicity without pikestaff plainness. Fireplaces, treated as sources of heat rather than dramatic features, were usually of brick, with a redwood board for a mantel. They often had a deep redwood seat on one side.

As early as 1895 he began to cut back the eaves above windows and to use clerestories. Three large grouped windows often dissolved the upper half of the gable end. Living rooms opened to protected gardens, or on the west to pergolas. When the wall separating dining from living room was removed, all Berkeley was shocked.

By 1905 and 1906 the two trends in his domestic work began to merge. In the 1906 Tufts house, San Anselmo, the simpler forms were still evident, and the development was rather in the refinement of interior detailing. Examples of this were the well-considered lighting fixtures; one was a light well with openings in the hall, dining and living room and the broom closet.

The evolution of Maybeck's personal forms could be seen in the Roos and Goslinsky houses in San Francisco, both built in 1909. The emphasis was still on the roof but there was greater concentration of forms, and ornament was developed on wall surfaces and balcony rails.

Although all of these houses have been in constant use 50 to 60 years, many have undergone few changes. In the Tufts house, built on an up-slope, the wide porch off the living room, with its panoramic view, was a forecast of the decks used in houses today. Three generations of children have grown up in the Schneider house in Berkeley. A plain table of redwood boards with 4 by 4-inch sanded redwood legs is still in use in the dining room, which is open to the living room and the view of the Bay through its French doors.

Charles Keeler, an early client, published a book in 1904 called *The Simple Home* which listed many of Maybeck's practices in wood.

The surface of rough sawn boards or timbers was slightly charred to produce a soft brown color and wavy texture; redwood was treated with sulphate of iron to turn it a silver gray; rough boards were also colored with soft green creosote stain to give a subdued and mossy effect; other stains were deep blue-green, ochre or chocolate. Dutch leaf metal or gold paint was applied in ornamental designs on wood.

The redwood board and batten walls were smooth and rarely decorated. In the 1920 Hunt residence, however, the battens were waxed and the boards left natural to give a rhythm of mat and shine to the walls. Maybeck found dozens of ways to decorate the truss work without violating the nature of the wood; members were multiplied, profiled, the ends carved or colored. He often used two different width boards in the open ceiling and stained the narrower boards a moss green or dull red. This striped effect led the eye up.

Wright expressed the modern house in a horizontality learned from the Japanese; Maybeck with a Gothic verticality. Height was the key to his planning. "He liked plenty of room up there," one of his carpenters remarked. The truss work of many a house was a minor masterpiece even though some trusses were constructed without detail drawings. Maybeck's daughter, Kerna Gannon, said about several houses, "he got into the peak and worked them out." But often there were "reams of details, to the smallest cut."

Maybeck's most urbane residence was the half-timbered house for department store owner Leon L. Roos, San Francisco, 1909. The site was a corner lot on Jackson Street. →

← *Three-and-one-half-story Goslinsky house, San Francisco, 1909, on a 25-foot lot. Here Maybeck's personal forms —which arose out of plan and a desire for adequate daylighting—dominated Gothic revival and Bay Region shingle influences. The house cost $6800.*

←

Detail of the Goslinsky house, showing flamboyant Gothic tracery in a screen for a window, and a Byzantine downspout in copper.

→
Double doors covered with antique amethyst velvet were set into wide panels of redwood in the entrance hall of the Roos house. Screens of redwood and velvet—which closed off the living room from the hall—slid into a pocket in the wall.

Maybeck looked for various ways to "age" stucco walls. He threw pails of muddy water onto new walls; he graduated their color from light to dark, with darker tones up under the eaves. The walls of the Lawson porches were once a Roman red; the dome of the rotunda of the Palace of Fine Arts is still a velvety burnt orange; the walls of the Kennedy house in Berkeley have a sunset glow in their various earth colors. When in 1928 it was time to spray the walls of his Packard Agency in Oakland, Maybeck and his client, Earle C. Anthony, rigged up a telephone between the building and an island on a small lake facing it. From the island Maybeck watched the color as it was applied, as well as its reflection in the lake; from time to time he telephoned directions for lightening or darkening the tone. When the colored Gunite was shot onto the walls of the Anthony house in Los Angeles, Maybeck was ill; however, he was carried to the scene and watched the operations from a cot set up in the garden.

His last experiment in color for stucco walls was a polychrome paint. Various colors—often green, gold and rust—were spattered from a brush onto the surfaces, and the intensity of the combined colors varied with the orientation of the wall. Today there is only one house painter left in the Bay Region who knows Maybeck's technique, and his prices are exorbitant.

Maybeck also varied the color and texture of floors by pouring strips of red or gray magnesite between every fourth floor board in two houses.

Maybeck's earlier fireplaces were of modest size but the later ones had baronial proportions. Many of his original drawings, still in existence, are too bulky to lie flat in a file; among the pages are full-scale drawings of fireplaces on folded sheets of tracing paper. These were developed on the job in cardboard, and later in plywood. Maybeck often stopped construction while a carpenter held up the boards in position; if he wasn't satisfied, he restudied the design. Maybeck practiced architecture as if it were a craft, constantly revising—in order to bring closer together the possibility and the actuality. This accounts to a large degree for his successes in blending unrelated styles.

The blending revealed a master storyteller who mixed fact with fiction so boldly that the whole had the dimension of truth. One feels that

Wyntoon, the castle for Mrs. Hearst on McCloud River, 1902, cost $100,000.

he must have invented the people to live in some of his houses. It is hard to believe that a client existed outside Maybeck's imagination for Wyntoon, his castle on the McCloud River, or for his reinforced concrete house of 1907. Wyntoon was commissioned by Mrs. Hearst, and the 1907 house by Prof. A. C. Lawson, a geologist whose advice was sought in the placing of the foundations of the Golden Gate Bridge.

Wyntoon was built in 1902 at a cost of $100,000—a sudden change from the $4,000 to $5,000 houses Maybeck had been building for artists and university professors. To design space for Mrs. Hearst's art objects was a hazard to one who looked upon architecture itself as a major art. Maybeck's love of drama was brought into full play in the castle of rubble stone; its complex of roofs built up to a tower with a pagoda roof. Those who remember Wyntoon before it was destroyed by fire speak of the high narrow, stone-walled living room as pure fantasy—with its great free-standing fireplace silhouetted

The living room with its free-standing fireplace silhouetted against a stained glass window was Maybeck's dramatic interpretation of Gothic style.

against an arch filled with stained glass. The Gothic proportions of the living room, with a beautiful waste space "up there," and the jagged skyline came out of no text book.

Although reinforced concrete had been used on the West Coast by E. L. Ransome during the last quarter of the nineteenth century, in 1907 it was still in an early stage of development. Ransome had reinforced small concrete buildings with wire cable and hoop iron. This had led to the development of reinforcing rods, used in the 1889 Stanford Museum in Palo Alto. After the 1906 earthquake and fire, Maybeck looked for a system of construction that would withstand seismic forces. In his 1907 Lawson house in Berkeley, he used monolithic concrete construction. The roof was a thin concrete slab with a low pitch.

This was the same year that Gill turned to the use of concrete in the Laughlin house. (His first monolithic construction came in 1908.) The two houses bear comparison. Maybeck's chief concern was to develop ornament that would blend with concrete, while Gill was content to enjoy the clean surfaces of the walls. (See page 67.)

In the Lawson house light necklaces of colored stones adorned the second-story walls and the fascias of the overhanging slab; around the double arches of the recessed porches were stylized patterns of acanthus leaves in sgraffito. There were no projections over the windows or French doors to the garden, but a round canopy sheltered the entrance door, at the side of the house.

An appreciation for the material was shown in the use of the arch for second-floor openings, and the relating of these to round shower room windows and a vertical row of round vents in the first-floor wall. Narrowness and height were absent; the house was Roman in conception, but modern in execution.

Maybeck related the house to the garden by a series of free-standing columns topped by individual pergolas, in which stick was piled upon stick as in the Christian Science Church. A pergolaed walk in the rear also stood free of the house and led to a pavilion.

His feeling for concrete was also evident in the interiors, where wide arched doors led from one room to another. Among the many materials Maybeck tried out in the interior rooms was milk white Vitrolite for the walls of a bathroom.

The Lawson house, Berkeley, 1907, Maybeck's first work in reinforced concrete, was of monolithic construction.

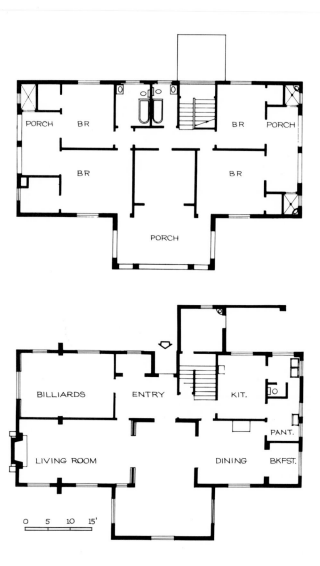

View from the balcony of the Lawson house, looking toward a pergola and pavilion at the rear. The wood applique on the fascia of the pavilion was in colors.

Rear elevation of the Lawson house, shown under construction. Diamond-shaped patterns in colored stones decorated the upper walls; murals covered the space around the arched openings of the porch.

View of the garden side of the Lawson house showing a rail that was added to the balcony. Designed by Maybeck, the rail was once a double garden gate.

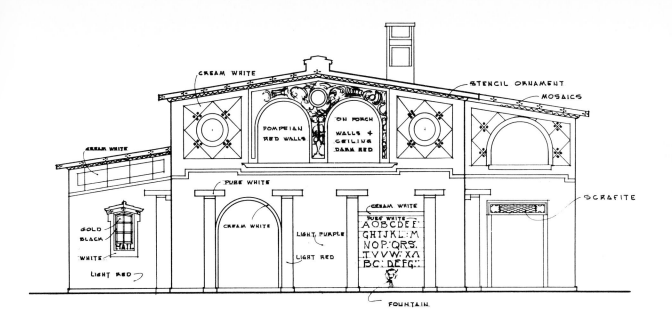

CREAM WHITE

STENCIL ORNAMENT

MOSAICS

CREAM WHITE

POMPEIAN
RED WALLS

ON PORCH
WALLS +
CEILING
DARK RED

SCRAFITE

PURE WHITE

GOLD
BLACK

CREAM WHITE

MAIL

WHITE

LIGHT PURPLE

LIGHT RED

LIGHT RED

CREAM WHITE
PURE WHITE
A OBCDEE
GHIJKL M
NOP QRS.
TVVW XA
BC DEFG

FOUNTAIN

In 1910, when Maybeck was almost 50, five women of the congregation of the First Church of Christ, Scientist came one day to talk to him. They wanted, he recalled, "a church that would look like a church" and built of materials "that are what they claim to be, not imitations." Maybeck, whose religious feeling embraced everything, asked about their religion. The sincerity with which they spoke reminded him of the faith of the men who had built the early Romanesque churches in the south of France.

Maybeck began to wonder how he could "put himself in the boots of a fellow in the twelfth century," as he described it. He was certain of one thing: the man of the Middle Ages would use "the most modern materials he could lay his hands on," and would combine them in such a way as to express the spirit of his faith.

After Maybeck had found what he wanted to say, he looked among the common materials— the natural ones and the fabricated ones. From industry he took asbestos panels and factory sash; cement and local redwood completed his list for the structure. He cast concrete in hexagonal columns for the loggia to the left of the portico; against these he played rough redwood columns. To the right was a row of freestanding square fluted columns also of cast concrete; on top of each was a single complex trellis structure, which brought wistaria vines into the architectural composition. The Romanesque capitals were in the spirit of those in Ste. Madeleine's at Vezelay. Many castings were made before Maybeck was satisfied. "He had great knowledge of what he wanted," according to Anthony Tovani, who made the castings. The capitals were one of the loveliest passages in Maybeck's work—the figures of carollers in high relief set a joyous theme which ruled the spirit of the entire church.

Asbestos panels formed a surfacing material for exterior walls; they were fastened to the frame in a rhythm of diamond-shaped pieces of red asbestos. Maybeck redivided the vertical divisions of the factory sash to give them the character of a Japanese screen, and inserted handmade glass of warm flesh tones.

Without towers or spires, he led the eye up, from the gently pitched roof covering the portico, from one hovering roof to a higher one, and finally to a modest cupola. It was a broad and friendly exterior, whose only thin verticals were the cast concrete tracery of the two great windows, and the delicate lines of the factory sash.

The directness with which Maybeck spanned the Greek cross plan was unexpected for one who loved height. Hinged trusses cut diagonally across the nave; the springings were four decorated concrete columns. The vertical members between the upper and lower chord were pierced with Gothic tracery outlined in gold.

Byzantine-inspired ornament on the capitals was picked out in gold, blue and red; designs were stencilled on rough-sawn redwood brackets in colors so subdued that color and texture were fused. There were endless lovely small details— the floral designs inscribed in the two cast concrete readers' stands; the hanging steel light bowls—pierced with a pattern of quatrefoils— above the pews; the cross-form lights of 4 by 4-inch redwood in the Fireplace Room; the multiplication of members in the open truss of the Fireplace Room, originally the Sunday School.

Maybeck moved with confidence from Renaissance plan to flamboyant Gothic tracery, from Romanesque columns to Japanese timber work, to Byzantine decoration. No one has ever carried the burden of the past more weightlessly.

(Text continued on page 37.)

→
Christian Science Church, Berkeley, 1910. Romanesque columns, to the right of the portico, were conceived as sculpture; they were topped by airy trellises planned to receive vines.

Sketch of front door handle (left).

OFFICE
2619

Side view and detail, Christian Science Church. Maybeck called this church—recognized today as one of the great works of modern architecture—a creation in the spirit of the past; in it he used only the most modern industrial materials available. The novelty of factory sash and asbestos panels has faded; there remains only Maybeck's incomparable skill in composing them into an enduring piece of architecture.

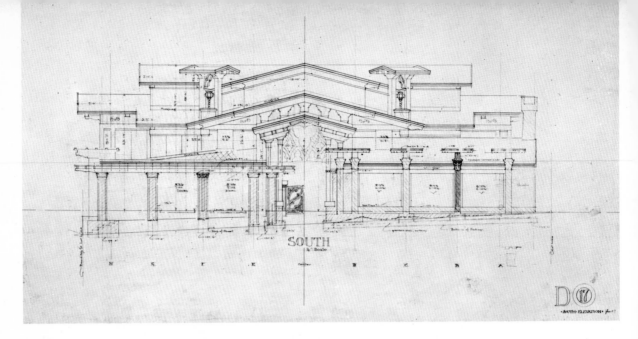

SOUTH

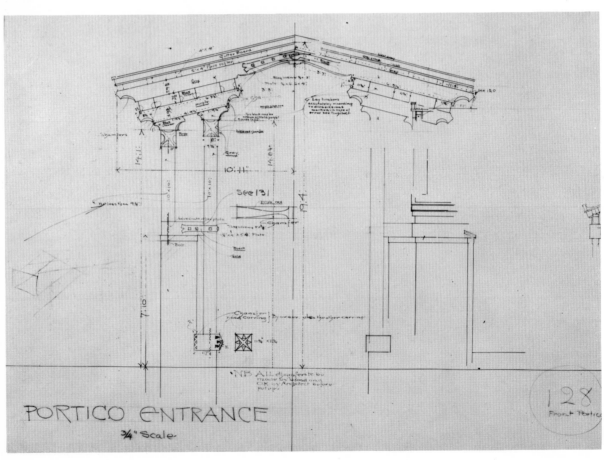

PORTICO ENTRANCE
3/4" Scale

View of portico entrance. The portico, in the spirit of a Japanese shrine, was detached from the rest of the building to admit light at the entrance. In contrast to the height of the portico, the entrance was low; the exposed wood structure was a preparation for the great hinged truss of the main room.

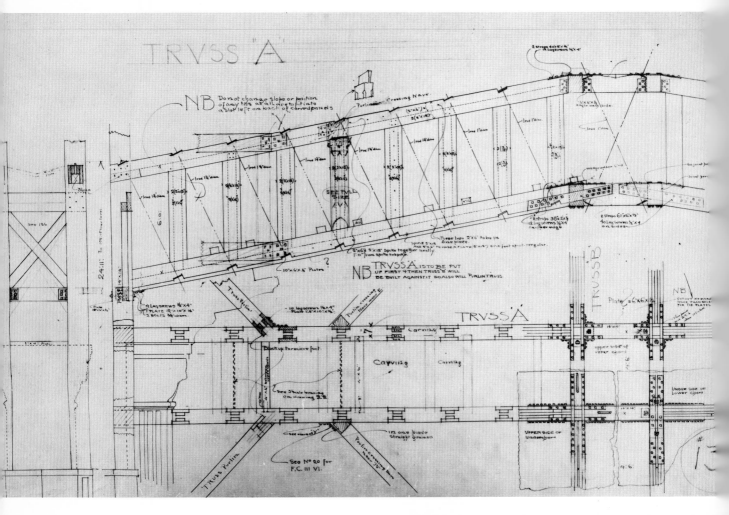

Interior, Christian Science Church, as seen from the entrance. The pulpit and cast concrete readers' stands were at the west end of the nave. Panels of Gothic tracery in gold were inserted between the upper and lower chords of the hinged arch, and rich designs picked out on the rough wood in blue, red and gold. Pierced light bowls were of hammered steel.

Intersection of the truss which spanned the Greek cross plan.

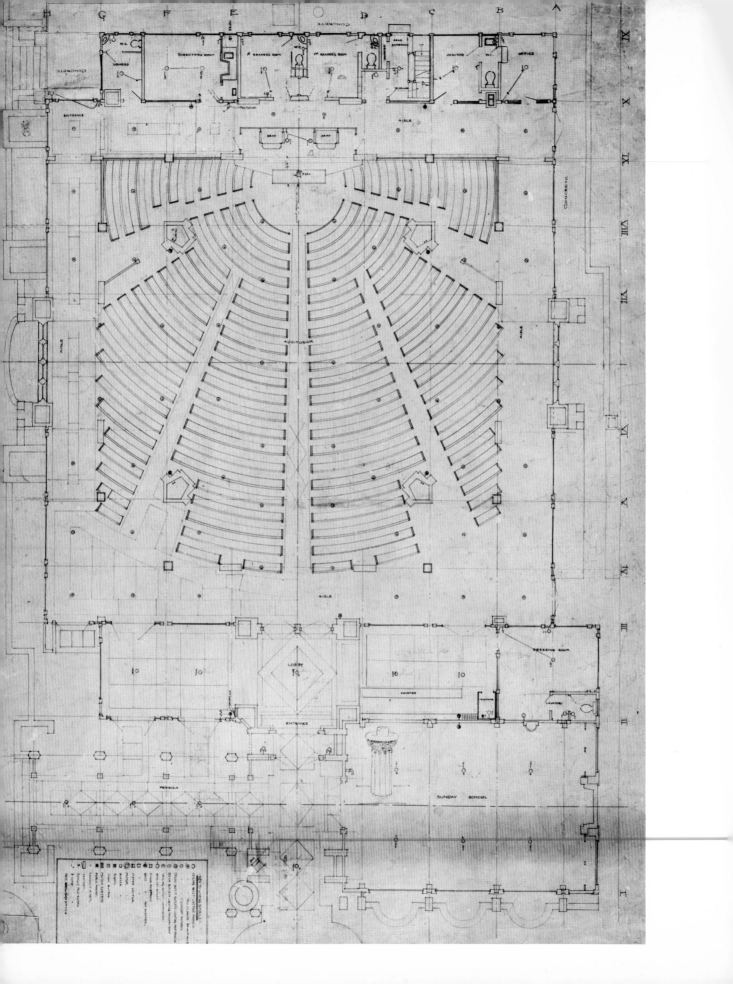

Interior, Christian Science Church, as seen from one of the readers' stands. The cast concrete columns, from which the arched truss sprang, contained the duct system.

Main floor plan, Christian Science Church. Seating arrangement was changed as shown in photograph.

Copyright Roy Flamm

Fireplace Room (formerly the Sunday School), Christian Science Church. Patterns on the tripled beams were in color. The light fixtures were 4 by 4-inch redwood capped with hammered brass.

→

The formwork of the concrete fireplace repeated the rhythm of the board and battens of the Fireplace Room. The standard steel factory sash, used throughout for windows, was filled with pale amber handmade glass.

←

In 1929 a new Sunday School wing was added to the church by Maybeck in association with Henry Gutterson. The portico was to the north of the main entrance to the church.

After the design of the Christian Science Church, Maybeck's affairs began to go badly. Unlike Charles Sumner Greene, also a consummate artist, whose letters to his broker testify to considerable business acumen, Maybeck was as innocent as a babe in matters of money. Over a period of thirty-five years or more he had three different offices in San Francisco, and commuted there from Berkeley, but the rewards were small. Mrs. Maybeck took over the bookkeeping several years after their marriage; she paid all the bills, and her brother, Mark White, superintended the construction of buildings. Nevertheless, as Maybeck's son, Wallen Maybeck, told me, "When the architect's fee was 8 per cent it was used up before a job was completed, and when the fee was raised to 10 per cent it still evaporated. Father would change and change a house, and Mother would go out and borrow again." Maybeck's one sign of brilliance in business was the purchase of four acres of land in the Berkeley hills; he was sure that the town would grow in that direction. Mrs. Maybeck thought the land was just another loss, but according to Wallen it saved the family. "When the sheriff was around the corner, another lot would be sold."

In 1912 when the plans for the Panama Pacific International Exposition were being discussed, Maybeck was not invited to participate. He was automatically excluded because he had executed no large buildings. When he recalled the incident in 1950 he said, "I hadn't even done a warehouse. However, Mrs. Maybeck ripped the boys up and down the back with letters." Her message was: give Ben a job.

The head of the architectural committee was Willis Polk, one of Maybeck's former students who in 1918 designed the famous glass curtain Hallidie Building in San Francisco. He hired Maybeck as a draftsman on an hourly basis to coordinate work in the Joy Zone. The Palace of Fine Arts had been assigned to Polk but since he was busy, he asked the draftsmen in the Exposition office to put their minds to work on a scheme.

Maybeck knew the grounds well from frequent inspections in the Joy Zone. He remembered a depression in the land in which water had collected and went to investigate. He thought of dredging out a lagoon at this spot, and making it a part of the architectural scheme

Palace of Fine Arts, San Francisco, 1915. Two elliptical colonnades on either side of the rotunda followed the curve of the lagoon. Maybeck conceived the structures not only as forms against the sky but also as forms reflected in water—the source of their ageless charm.

of the Palace of Fine Arts. His idea was a structure that would be as beautiful reflected in the water as it was against the sky.

With his usual loose and atmospheric approach to preliminary design, he sketched a gallery, an elliptical colonnade and rotunda in charcoal. At the back of his mind was the memory of Piranesi engravings; it was this melancholy note in architecture and gardening that he strove to attain. In an introduction to Maybeck's booklet, *The Palace of Fine Arts and Lagoon, Panama Pacific Exposition, 1915,* Frank Morton Todd wrote that Maybeck's theme was a building of vanquished grandeur, in which "willows and acacias choked its portals, grasses dug into its urns and ivy overran its cornices and dimmed its lines."

The sketch was passed along by Polk to other members of the Architectural Commission; the person most impressed by the sketch was Henry Bacon of New York, designer of the Lincoln Memorial. "You will hear of this some day," he promised Maybeck.

Because of Bacon's interest in the design, Maybeck's scheme for the Palace of Fine Arts was adopted. Willis Polk, unwilling to be the author of something that was not his, stepped aside and generously gave Maybeck full charge of the work. However, Maybeck continued to be paid his draftsman's wage. "I didn't get rich on that job," he said.

All the buildings at the Exposition were designed in the neo-classical style made famous by the Columbian Exposition. In his booklet Maybeck wrote that he had arrived at his forms and details as one "matches the color of a ribbon with a sample in his hand . . . You do the same with architecture. You examine an historic form and you see whether the effect it produces in your mind matches the feeling you are trying to portray."

The orange octagonal rotunda was set at the center of the composition; on either side were two detached peristyles made of an imitation travertine marble, which had been developed for repair work on the Pennsylvania Station in New York. The peristyle repeated the curve of the art gallery and followed the shore line of the lagoon. The rotunda dominated the entire landscape.

The guidebook, *The Architecture and Landscape Gardening of the Exposition,* stated

"Of all the wonderful effects of the Exposition grounds none is so full of haunting beauty as the vistas afforded by the Palace of Fine Arts . . . By the indirect system of illumination, an effect as of strong moonlight is produced and from concealed sources under cornices and behind columns, a soft reflected radiance pervades peristyle and rotunda."

In an introduction to the exposition guide, Louis Christian Mullgardt, another pioneer of western modern architecture, and a member of the Architectural Commission, also commented on the Palace of Fine Arts, "The entire composition bespeaks the mind of a romanticist whose productions are swayed more by nature's glories than by scholastic tradition."

Maybeck received a citation from the American Institute of Architects for the Palace of Fine Arts. Before the Exposition closed there was a movement to save Maybeck's group from demolition. The Contractors' Association considered it a hazard and wrote at length in *Architect and Engineer,* November, 1915, on why the buildings would not stand up. Maybeck replied in the same issue: "The Palace of Fine Arts is on United States property; eight columns and a piece of the altar are on Lyon Street, San Francisco property. The foundation is on piles and good soil. The walls are of cement. The roof is cement and glass. The building is absolutely fireproof. The construction of the rotunda and colonnade is of wood, very heavy on account of the great concentration of the loads. The colonnade was calculated to carry tons of wet earth, which was never put on the roof. The Palace of Fine Arts was constructed by the best engineers the Panama Pacific International Exposition could find; if anything, it is too strong. If San Francisco were shaken by an earthquake, the Palace of Fine Arts would be the last to go. The staff work is cast. It is made of nephi plaster and wood fiber; it is not put on with a trowel as on bungalows, but is stratified in the casting, like stone, and will not peel off. If the Palace of Fine Arts were in another climate the ornamental surface would soon be destroyed by ice and snow and heat, but in San Francisco Mission Dolores still stands, made of mud and straw. If left absolutely alone the Palace of Fine Arts will outlast us. It has cost $700,000."

But both the contractors and Maybeck were mistaken. The buildings stood up but the orna-

The peristyle walk in the Palace of Fine Arts group. At the right is the curved wall of the palace itself where paintings were hung. Alternating with the massed green of shrubs and plants against the wall are niches holding sculpture. The square Roman urns are by William Gladstone Merchant, who succeeded Maybeck.

The Chick house, nestled among live oaks, was lighted by banks of windows under the wide eaves.

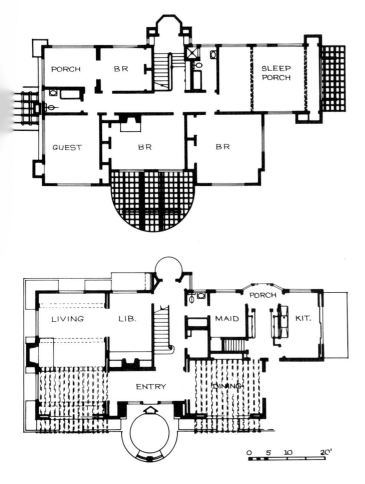

View of the Chick house, Berkeley, 1913, showing trellis. By piling stick upon stick Maybeck gave his trellises substance and depth; the play of light through them enriched many an eave line.

ment began to crumble, and as in Maybeck's words, "nature outgrew the gardener's stiffening care," he watched the decay with pleasure. This was what he had been after in the first place—a ruins. At the end of the first World War, Willis Polk—in accepting a post with the city's Memorial and Monument Committee—suggested that the Palace of Fine Arts be rebuilt of permanent materials as a war memorial. Polk said that the buildings "seem to me always holding out mythical hands in a pitiful appeal for restoration, perpetuation." Nothing came of Polk's proposal.

As the years passed and time and weather continued their destructive work, the colonnade and rotunda grew dearer to the hearts of San Franciscans. But in 1958 a bond issue to rebuild was voted down, and it seemed destined for destruction. However, in 1959 Walter Johnson, a San Francisco resident, gave $2 million to save the structures; with $2 million more added by the state of California, the Palace of Fine Arts will be rebuilt from original plans on file in the University of California architectural library.

In the meantime, from across the lagoon where the colonnade and rotunda are twice seen, once in sky, once in water, time has dimmed their lines to the softness of Maybeck's original charcoal drawing.

Two of Maybeck's fine works in shingle in his middle period were the 1913 Chick house in Berkeley and the 1917 Bingham house in Montecito. The Chick house was developed under a gable roof, with particular emphasis on the upper half of the gable ends; it extended two feet beyond the first floor, forming a bonnet around the bank of second-floor windows. The material as well as the plane was changed— vertical redwood boards were used as surfacing for the gable ends of the second floor, the battens varying between flat and rounded ones. The interior space of the projections at the four corners was developed as bedroom closets.

The fine trellising at the eave line tied the house into the green of the oaks, while the notching and stacking of the shingles at the foundation line and on the arch of a door related the work to indigenous carpentry. The house had an air of simple elegance. In the living room a huge fireplace was flanked on either side by floor-to-ceiling French doors so that it appeared to be set in a glass wall—a daring effect for 1913.

43

Entrance, Chick house.

The second-floor hall of the Chick house led to a balcony. The wooden rail was pierced with quatrefoils, Maybeck's favorite Gothic detail.

A concrete and redwood fireplace was set in a glass wall of the Chick house living room. The room was oriented toward a wooded canyon. Note the cove lighting. →

Cove lighting further enhanced the drama.

Maybeck's great house in Montecito for A. E. Bingham had in its sprawling plan and wide eaves a certain kinship to the Greenes, whose work Maybeck knew through the Thorsen residence in Berkeley. The resemblance was, however, superficial. Maybeck used wide eaves because of the Southern California climate. However, he continued his practice of cutting back the eaves, in this case above the bank of windows on the third floor play room.

The main block of the house was two and three floors, with two one-story wings. The one-story living room was opened by large glass areas on the sides to wide lawns, and at the west end to a pergola poised on enormous tapered stone pillars. Between the living room and terrace was a large arched door whose glass slid into the wall.

Despite the overly ornate fireplace, the living room was one of the most gracious Maybeck designed. Like the Chick house, it had cove lighting. Stencilled silks and blue gauze applied over gold paint gave a particularly rich effect to the ceiling. Rough grass cloth contrasted with the flush paneling of ash boards. Today the untreated light wood gives the room an astonishingly contemporary air.

Before the Exposition opened, Europe was at war, and the growth of the lumber industry and shipping in the west brought two commissions somewhat similar in nature. One was the layout of a town, Brookings, Oregon, in 1914, for Brookings Lumber Company. The University library contains Maybeck's complete drawings for the layout of the town of 2500. Among them are designs for a concrete bank, a school, cottages for workmen and larger houses for officials. The only building executed was a temporary wooden dormitory for workmen. With the end of the war the rest of the project was abandoned.

The second commission came in 1917 as a result of Maybeck's appointment as a Supervising Architect to the United States Shipping Board. His work was confined to the area around San Francisco; his sole assignment was to lay out a new town, Clyde, near Port Chicago, to take care

Eaves of the Bingham house, Montecito, 1917, were cut away above the banked windows of the third-floor playroom and on the north side (left); a sliding glass door opened the one-story living room to a pergola.

←

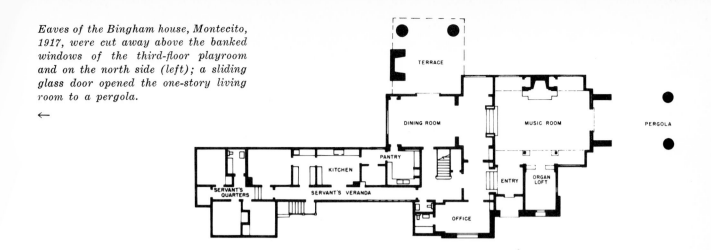

The shingled Bingham house was reminiscent of the Greenes' work. Instead of wide covered porches, Maybeck developed terraces on the south and west sides of the house.

of the enormous increase in employees in the shipyards. However, the grid layout of the streets (imposed on the plan before Maybeck's arrival) shows less of his influence than does the design of a hotel and some of the 200 or more houses. The plans for all the buildings were drawn in the office of Acting Architect George Applegarth, who later designed the Palace of the Legion of Honor and the Spreckles mansion. There was nothing in Applegarth's later work that referred in any way to the Clyde hotel. To be a supervising architect obviously was an opportunity for Maybeck to direct the design.

The hotel was Maybeck's only building that showed any Sullivanesque traits. The wide, flat cornices, supported by paired brackets, floated above a frieze of stylized garlands in wood applique. On the facade long narrow units of steel factory sash were recessed and the reveal extended the entire 30-foot height of the building. The impression was of openness between massive columns.

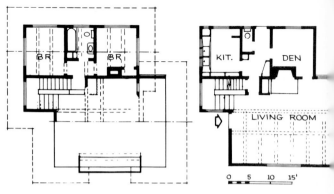

The enormous lounge, the full height of the facade, was paneled in 14-inch redwood boards; off the lounge were wide stairs leading by slow stages to the upper floors. The eaves were cut away above each bedroom window and the rhythm of the broken eaves was repeated in shadows on wall or ground.

Today the deserted hotel stands among weeds and rubble, disintegrating from neglect. It has the sort of ageless splendor that pervades the Palace of Fine Arts, but no benefactor has yet arisen to restore it.

Soon after the end of the war Maybeck executed several small but significant commissions. They revealed no change in his approach to work. In the 1919 Matheuson house two broad gabled roofs were gathered at one end of the house, under a roof with an off-center ridge, with remarkable grace. The first-floor walls were of stucco, and the upper ones of rough redwood boards were stained a moss green. The 1919 Forest Hill Clubhouse with its excellent treatment of wall planes related back to the 1899 Town and Gown Clubhouse; the scalloped fascia was similar to one on the Forest Hill School at Carmel. Redwood boards, 1 by 4 inches, were set within panels of 1 by 8-inch redwood to give a half-timbered effect.

In 1923 Maybeck designed some broad, low

The Matheuson house, Berkeley, 1919, was one of the finest examples of Maybeck's ability to cut back eaves and swing them up while maintaining an uncomplicated roof structure.

←

Dormitories of the hotel at Clyde, built before the recreation hall, could accommodate 200 men. Note the shadow patterns of cutouts in the eave line.

Reception hall, hotel at Clyde, 1917. The hotel, built to house wartime shipping employees, was a forerunner of federal housing. A T-shaped plan placed the two-story hall at right angles to dormitories. The stepped roof followed stairs leading to hall. Despite its monumental scale, the building had friendliness.

←

Forest Hill Club, San Francisco, 1917.

mountain cabins for Glen Alpine Lodge on Lake Tahoe. He placed factory sash between massive tapering granite piers; for roofing material he bent long sheets of corrugated iron over the roof peak. These delightfully open cabins were reminiscent of a mountain lodge for the 1915 Sierra Club. The very richness of Maybeck's imagination and the diversity of his style makes recognition of familiar details all the more pleasurable.

The disastrous fire in Berkeley in 1923 destroyed many of Maybeck's houses, and he turned again to concrete. However, he did not use monolithic construction as in the 1907 Lawson house. In search of a cheap fireproof surfacing material, he tried coating burlap sacks with a foamy concrete mixture called "Bubble Stone." This material, invented by a Berkeley man, was produced by mixing chemicals with cement; it was so light in weight that a mass the size of a bale of hay could be lifted by one man.

Maybeck's production of Bubble Stone has been described by Jack Hillmer, San Francisco architect, who, in 1959, with Roy Flamm, photographer, prepared the first large exhibition of Maybeck's work. The water and chemicals were mixed in an old washing machine, then Maybeck folded cement and sand mortar (without aggregate) into the froth "like adding sugar to whipped cream." Wet burlap sacks dipped into the mixture came out with about an inch of foamy concrete adhering to them.

The coated sacks were then nailed to the studs and sheathing of a cottage, in which factory sash served as windows and as French doors to the garden. The total cost of the cottage was $600. It is still in use today, although the cement is chipping away from the sacks.

After the 1923 fire Maybeck seldom used wood in the Berkeley hills; he began to develop a style in stucco and tile. The Jeralemon and the McMurray houses, both built immediately after the fire, were important not only for their plastic forms of semi-fireproof materials but also for inventive plan and detail. The entrance to the Jeralemon house was a hyphen between the main house and a studio. Both houses had combined living and dining rooms, and were the first houses with ranges set into the kitchen work counters.

Although Maybeck's work began to taper off,

Glen Alpine cabins, Lake Tahoe, 1923, revealed Maybeck's genius in the integration of the buildings into the rugged site, the rhythm and logic of the forms, and the direct use of industrial materials—corrugated iron for roofs, and metal factory sash and doors for the interspaces between the enormous granite piers.

The Kennedy house, Berkeley, 1923, had a curved street-front wall and ramp. To give the concrete a mellowness of age the walls were colored in tones graduating from soft peach to burnt orange.

in 1926, at the age of 65, he found in Earle C. Anthony a client who believed, even more than Maybeck did, in the principle of mixing styles. This led to some of his largest commissions, two Packard showrooms in San Francisco and Oakland and the interior for one in Los Angeles. But the financial plum was the Anthony house.

"Father was afraid of money," Wallen Maybeck told me; what Maybeck may have been afraid of was the architectural self-indulgence to which money could lead. Each one of the Anthony commissions had grandiosity in which there was no relationship to the small library for Carmel that Maybeck did the same year. However self-indulgent the interiors of the showrooms may have been, Maybeck was incapable of self-infatuation. Arches sprang from marble columns five feet in diameter; their plaster collars were coarse and strong. Columns of red Nubidian marble, cored with steel, were surmounted by capitals resembling four sets of giant pulleys. Ceilings were of pecky cypress timbers; floors were of green tile. These symbols of power were woven into a single theme—commerce—by one who was innocent of the subject. The work for Anthony was a fantasy of Rome Unvanquished, but Rome made believable by Maybeck's authority with color and materials.

Before and during the period Maybeck was designing their 1927 medieval castle in Los Angeles, the Anthonys traveled in Europe seven times gathering photographs of Gothic castles. They brought home $35,000 worth of stone from Caen, roof tile from Barcelona, and samples of fabrics.

W. P. Casson, Anthony's assistant, wrote in his notes on the house that the variety of architectural forms and details from various periods were combined to "reflect the changes, additions and variances which would have been wrought by dozens of succeeding generations. This tower might have been added by the hand of a conqueror, that one by some gentler baron so that his chatelaine might view the countryside. This section seems the work of some wandering Spanish mason, while only a Tudor craftsman would have designed these leaded windows . . ."

The house cost half a million dollars. Built on flat ground, there were 21 changes in levels. The living room was 35 feet high, walls of Caen stone were 5 feet thick and floors were of rough-

The Packard Agency, Oakland, 1928, designed for Earle C. Anthony, reflected Romanesque forms in a lake.

53

hewn oak timbers. One door weighed 1,500 pounds; it was of solid walnut and had a castle key for a handle. Gargoyles, portcullis spikes, balustrades, moldings and staircases were copied from Anthony's photograph album. In the garage were seven Packards.

The authentic Gothic chapel and the battlements crowned with a Norman tower had characteristic Maybeck details. The living room windows were 8 feet wide and 18 feet high; the lower sections slid not only sideways for passage but also upward in order to open the room to the patio.

In contrast, the little library in Carmel contained more creative thought. An enormous fireplace in one wall of the long, narrow reading room was flanked by low seats and circled by wicker chairs. Although fluorescent lights have replaced the incandescent bulbs that Maybeck hung from long, brightly colored, frizzed cotton ropes, the room still creates a fine sense of leisure.

In 1927 Maybeck worked in association with Julia Morgan on the Hearst Memorial Gymnasium for Women, and in 1929 with Henry Gutterson on a Sunday School for the Christian Science Church. His last important commission was for the layout and buildings of The Principia College campus. Originally planned, in 1923, for St. Louis, the site was later changed to Elsah, Illinois, and construction work was not started until 1938. The eight buildings completed were in Maybeck's Tudor style, executed in reinforced concrete which he left for the most part unsurfaced. He did not supervise the work; although there were unmistakable marks of Maybeck's creativity, the buildings had little of the vigor of the man who had once, in the phrase of the poet Eli Seigel, "traveled in common darkness to shed uncommon light."

Maybeck continued to go to his office until 1942 when he was 80 years old. He was succeeded by William Gladstone Merchant, who at nineteen had worked for Maybeck as an assistant on the Palace of Fine Arts. The Maybecks spent the war years in Twainheart in a cabin he designed for them; it was built of cedar bark at a cost of $1,500.

While in Twainheart he worked on drawings of a proposed boulevard for San Francisco. Formerly he had been a member of the Berkeley City Planning Board; his drawings of a pro-

Entrance to the Anthony house was through a Norman tower. The insistence of the Anthonys upon authentic details left Maybeck little room to exercise his talent for paraphrasing past styles in his own design language.

View of the Anthony house, Los Angeles, 1927, from across a free-form pool, showing arched windows of dining room.

posed boulevard for Berkeley hung for some years in the office of the Planning Board.

At the end of the war he returned to Berkeley. Wearing a smock and a tam o'shanter, he often sat in the eucalyptus grove beside his house. From this vantage point he could see many of his sculptural chimneys on houses he had designed for the Berkeley hills. The double openings at the top of the chimneys syphoned out the air; they were his signature on a building. The chimneys were of many shapes and sizes but the formula was the same for all: the flue was one-tenth the size of the fireplace opening.

Near his home were the common gardens he had made a part of his planning; the groves of eucalyptus; the beautiful Rose Walk, which connected an upper with a lower street in the hills —examples of what Frederick Law Olmsted called "good outgoings . . . requisites of an attractive neighborhood."

Honors had begun to accumulate; in 1951 when he was 89, Maybeck received the Gold Medal of the American Institute of Architects, the highest honor it bestows.

He could not be idle; he spent his time building a model for a Unitarian Church for Berkeley, and even worked on a model of an airplane with perforated wings that flapped. He was happy to talk to visitors on most any subject, but the conversation invariably led him back to his childhood spent near Washington Square, and his days at the Beaux Arts. His six years in Paris, his visits to the South of France, and to Viollet-le-Duc's restorations of Romanesque buildings were clearer in his mind than the 250 or more buildings he had designed, and the early Gothic builders were closer than the people who sat opposite him in the garden chairs.

When old clients came to ask about adding a room or remodeling a kitchen in the style in which he had worked, he advised them, according to Gerard Hurley who lives in the 1921 Cedric Wright house, to "Make it good, make it new. That's what I tried to do when I built it."

Maybeck died on October 3, 1957. His name still remains on the directory in the lobby of the Rust Building on Post Street and on an office door. It is the office of William Gladstone Merchant, now a Regent of the University of California. The name is there because, Merchant said, "Maybeck didn't like the idea of retiring. I promised him he'd have an office as long as I was alive."

Maybeck's carpenter, Ivan Melvin, recalling Maybeck, said, "In his casket he wore his cap. He didn't look much different than he did during the depression when he called me over and said: 'You haven't anything to do and I haven't anything to do so we'll just build a house. We'll lay it out today.' We walked over his land and we found a spot and we laid it out. He wanted me to build a house too. 'Take some land, as little as you want or as much and pay me whenever you like.' He just sold the land by the foot.

"He was always trying something out," Melvin continued. "Once we tore down an electric stove in 1923 and built the rings into a tile counter and put the oven in the wall. He built a house once without any metal hinges. He built a house for his son Wallen with double concrete walls and put rice hulls between them. He could draw the prettiest picture of a stairway, sitting there with the drawing board on his lap, and I'd ask him what size posts to put in and he'd say, 'Six by sixes. Put in a few.' But if he took a notion to draw details he drew them perfect.

"He was a good man. He was a real common man. And he knew what he was looking for."

Hearst Memorial Gymnasium for Women, University of California, Berkeley, 1927, designed by Maybeck in association with Julia Morgan, a graduate of the Beaux Arts. The monumental building lacked the light airy touch of pergola or trellis, typical of Maybeck.

IRVING GILL

1870-1936

In 1890, Irving John Gill, the twenty-year-old son of a Syracuse, New York, building contractor set out for Chicago to work in the drafting room of Adler and Sullivan. This was his first step westward, one which led him two years later to San Diego, where he developed one of the few wholly original styles of architecture in the United States.

He had never met Sullivan, nor even written to him, but he was quite aware of his work, and like dozens of young architects with an independent way of thinking, he looked upon Sullivan's office as the only true school of architecture.

Gill had nothing to offer in the way of formal architectural training, indeed, his education had stopped with high school. The closest he had come to official architecture was a brief period in one of the offices in Syracuse. This may have prejudiced Sullivan in his favor, as Sullivan looked upon schooling as a mere facility for dipping in and out of books.

Gill had other virtues to recommend him beside his innocence of architectural styles. Poetic and mystical by nature, he had a sensitivity to form, an understanding of how a building is put together, and a passion for sim-

Window of the Christian Science Church, San Diego, 1904.

59

plifying. He firmly believed in the application of democracy to architecture. In addition, he was receptive to the faiths of a great teacher.

Sullivan described his relationship to his young draftsmen in a letter to Claude Bragdon, "I supply the yeast, so to speak, and allow the ferment to work in them."

It was the dawn of steel, and Chicago had begun to think in terms of expressed structure rather than literary architectural styles. With engineer and contractor pointing the way, Sullivan anticipated the others of his profession by integrating steel into architecture. But the lesson of steel offered by Chicago and Sullivan profited Gill only indirectly, for the vertical line had no application in San Diego where he did most of his work. His highest building there was the 1908 five-story Wilson Acton Hotel. From Sullivan he had learned to acknowledge and respect his material, whatever it was.

Of far greater value to him was Sullivan's preaching of freedom from Rome and the Renaissance. Sullivan turned the faces of the young men away from Europe and bade them look to Africa, a land of the serene wall, of earth forms, of decorative details.

Sullivan's office was a preparation, for defeat as well as success. The inevitable growth of modern architecture did not spare it from periods of eclipse. At the Columbian Exposition in Chicago Sullivan's Transportation Building was the only one that heralded the future; the others were designed in the neo-classical style set by the architectural committee.

The draftsman working on the plans of the Transportation Building was Frank Lloyd Wright, who was two years older than Gill. When Wright's son, Lloyd, was 20 years old, he went to work in Gill's drafting room.

Before the Exposition opened, Gill's health made it necessary for him to seek a warmer climate. But his two years with Sullivan had armored him with faith in his own thinking and enriched him with what Sullivan called "the luminous idea of simplicity." He had grasped the organic aspect of architecture, and regarded a building as a unified whole rather than a series of unrelated strands.

San Diego was well known in the East; after the Santa Fe Railway had laid tracks into the town in 1885, the population had doubled within a few years. Then the bubble burst, and by

1893, when Gill arrived, San Diego was feeling the depression of the mid-nineties. Most of the newcomers had packed up and left; the population was again around 17,000.

He found the country unspoiled and unself-conscious. "The west," he wrote in *The Craftsman,* "has an opportunity unparalleled in the history of the world, for it is the newest white page turned for registration." It awakened all his sensibilities. "In California we have the great wide plains, arched blue skies that are fresh chapters yet unwritten. We have noble mountains, lovely little hills and canyons waiting to hold the record of this generation's history, ideals, imagination, sense of romance and honesty."

He opened himself fully to all the things around him, such as the adobes, earth forms that gradually began to appear in his own structures; and Ramona's Marriage Place, with its U-shaped plan embracing a garden and closed at the end by a high wall. He called the single-wall redwood houses "lovable little camp houses . . . as natural a part of the foothills and canyons as the tawny mushroom or the gray stone." He described the missions, as "a most expressive medium of retaining tradition, history and romance, with their long, low lines, graceful arcades, tile roofs, bell towers, arched doorways, and walled gardens."

Gill's style grew out of what he found in Southern California. He added elements that were missing, and produced an architecture as uninsistent as the change of the seasons. His architecture was integrated into the past, the climate and the way of life so that it blended into the scene, as do the houses in a Cotswold village and in Tuscany. The fact that San Diego has something approaching a unity of style is due entirely to Gill, whose work was extensive and widely copied by contractors and various draftsmen who had been through his office.

It was an architecture of modesty, and repetition. The elements he repeated were those which his perceptive eye recognized as good; they had been tried and tried again until they reached the ideal of appropriateness. Gill was a conservator of the past, building always for the present, in new materials, with new methods evolved through arduous trial and error.

He was a romanticist whom time has shown to be a realist. His references to the missions in his work indicated a romantic regard for the past—rather than a sentimental attempt to recapture it. His expressions in light, color and the integration of house and garden were certainly romantic considerations.

The voice of the romantic poet was evident in his words: "We should build our house simple, plain and substantial as a boulder, then leave the ornamentation of it to Nature, who will tone it with lichens, chisel it with storms, make it gracious and friendly with vines and flower shadows as she does the stone in the meadow." (From *The Craftsman,* May, 1916.)

However, Gill left nothing to chance. He put to work certain principles of which he had a profound knowledge: the principle of the stone, which he translated into concrete; the principle of naturalness, which he used in his coordination of house and garden by pergolas, courts, patios and porches. He understood shadows and shadings, and they enhanced his walls, but when the vines are stripped away and the trees which cast shadows are uprooted, his sensitive forms remain.

Gill's first building in San Diego, the Normal School, 1895, gave little hint of his later creativity. Now demolished, it revealed only that he and the chairman of the board liked columns. But Gill never again used Ionic capitals. His later columns were strong and modest, with small bands and flat caps.

Other early works were also highly derivative in style. His Pickwick Theatre, 1904, looked as if he had laid tracing paper over Sullivan's Transportation Building and squeezed it into a 40-foot front. A fountain in the San Diego Plaza was reminiscent of the Coragic Monument of Lysicrates. But among Gill's sketches was another study for the Plaza fountain in a style very much his own. The client for both fountain and theatre was Louis Wilde for whom Gill, in 1919, planned a duplex in Coronado. His nephew, Louis J. Gill, later recalled that Wilde had said, "You build it and then I'll tell you where I want the doors and windows." Gill finally resigned the job. He walked out on one other occasion, when, in 1909, the congregation of the Christian Science Church, San Diego, decided to add a dome to his design.

The First Methodist Church, 1906, Gill's only attempt at Gothic architecture, was uninspired. Although it contained examples of good detail-

Wildacre, a house for Albert H. Olmsted in Newport, Rhode Island, was originally of unpainted shingles. Windows on the porch and in the hexagonal wing dropped into the parapet.

Birckhead house, Portsmouth, Rhode Island, 1902, was in the indigenous Shingle style.

ing, he was not at home in revival styles. As Louis Gill put it, "He didn't know one style from another," and this perhaps was his good fortune.

In 1898 Gill entered into a partnership with W. S. Hebbard. Out of their office came several amiable brick and half-timbered houses for San Diego and Coronado, all of them remarkable for their simple and direct use of redwood for interiors. In the McKenzie house of 1898, however, the walls were paneled with cherry wood shipped from Japan. (The present owner has ripped much of it out and papered the walls.)

Gill had a great deal to do with winning clients for the firm, for he had a broad handsome Irish face—his mother had been born in Ireland—and a sincere and straightforward way of speaking. His passion for dancing was perhaps a reaction to his strict Quaker upbringing; he often went to dances at the Coronado Hotel, where many easterners came to spend the winter months. There he met the Olmsted brothers, Frederick Law, Jr. and Albert, and their sister Marion, the sons and daughter of Frederick Law Olmsted, the famous park planner. Through the Olmsteds he was introduced to the wealthy and philanthropic Mason sisters, supporters of Tuskeegee Institute. As a result of the meeting, in 1902, Gill was commissioned to design a house for them, almost a mansion, in Newport, Rhode Island.

The house was a sensation in Newport, for thousands of feet of redwood were shipped to Newport to be used for the interiors. The mission influence was evident in the stucco walls, arches and red tile roof, but the scale was eastern and fashionable.

Gill was more successful with two other Rhode Island houses he designed the same year, the Birckhead house in Portsmouth and the Albert Olmsted house in Newport. In both he combined indigenous shingle work with California redwood interiors.

He also took other elements to the East such as the corner window, which he had first used in 1898 in the McKenzie house in Coronado. In several of his eastern houses he designed windows that dropped into a parapet wall, some of which still operate today.

After his success in the East, Gill returned to San Diego to find himself much sought after at home. In 1904 he designed a Christian Science

The Prairie style influence was evident in the Burnham house, San Diego, 1906. The brick was set inside frames of 12-inch redwood boards bolted to the stud frame.

Church, four residences and a theatre; he also built a house for himself that year.

He was still the young eclectic working mainly in brick and half-timbered style. In his own house, and in others built in 1905, he began to find his direction. But it was not until after 1906, when his partnership with Hebberd ended that he was on sure ground.

In the meantime his interiors had already developed in the direction of elimination and simplification typical of his mature work.

The redwood was used in dimensions large enough to register the nature of the wood, often 12-inch boards. Moldings were 2 by ¾-inch stock with sanded edges. Balustrades were made of square or rectangular sticking, a practice Gill continued up through the Dodge house of 1916. The only finish given the redwood was a sanding and hand polishing. He considered it a sacrilege to use oil, stain, or even wax on redwood. In the Christian Science Church he omitted moldings entirely, although they were added later, "to give (the church) a finished look." On the third floor of the Marston house he tried out doors made of five pieces of redwood, a step in the direction of his slab doors of 1907. He used magnesite in bathrooms and kitchens, and designed and cast in brass the hardware for all his buildings.

He was impatient with the infinite number of parts in a house; the wood frame seemed to him to be something hooked together, and he set himself to the business of simplifying structure, of eliminating, and making one piece do the work of ten. According to his nephew, "He was always trying to do something better. A window had 24 parts, and he designed one with four; then he found out the cost was the same. He looked for ways to apply plaster in his half-timbered houses to prevent it from shrinking away from the wood. He never stopped. He was never satisfied."

When he built a minimum house for himself in 1904, he experimented with structure. For some of the interior walls he tried out 1 by 4-inch studs, 4 inches apart, over which he placed diagonal lathing and plaster. The finished walls were 3 inches thick, and they tested equal to the 2 by 4-inch studs 16 inches on center, which made a 5½-inch wall. Plaster filled the openings between the 1 by 4-inch studs, so there were no spaces to act as fire flues.

The gate at the end of the Klauber
living porch led to a garden hedged in
by dark shiny mirror plants and twisted
bottle brush.

Service yard, Klauber house, San Diego,
1907. Note Gill's carefully scaled plane
surfaces.

Pleased with his experiment, Gill used the system for exterior walls and partitions in a house he designed in 1905 for Miss Alice Lee, the first of three commissions he undertook for her. The house was significant for another reason. The exterior was entirely of stucco, the form more compact, and the roof lower in pitch. Although he continued to design a few houses in half-timbered style, and did two shingled ones in 1906, he was moving toward the adobe forms of the mission builders, who had neither the time nor the tools to be other than frank.

Between the half-timbered and shingle houses and the ultimate ones in concrete, there were a number between 1906 and 1912 that showed the influence of the Prairie style in their strong horizontal lines and broad sheltering roofs.

At a time when houses were dim, Gill's were invariably bright. This came from the direct approach of the Chicago school to lighting office buildings. Sullivan's three-division window, with fixed glass in the center and an operating pane on each side, was typical of Gill's design.

By 1907, after ten years in California, he began to find what he was looking for. His changes in style always followed closely his changes in systems of construction. In the Melville Klauber and Homer Laughlin houses of that year he used concrete and hollow tile and furred out the interior walls. The tile was an excellent insulating material, and as the concrete did not shrink away from it there was less possibility of cracks.

The Klauber house had a gable roof with a slight Japanese curve in the pitch, while the roof of the Laughlin house was low and covered with tiles. Another change came in the interiors of the Laughlin house, where a minimum of wood was used. For about eight years Gill had coved his kitchen and bathroom walls into concrete floors; in the Laughlin house he carried this treatment throughout the entire house.

His inventiveness was applied to more than structure. A garbage disposal in the kitchen dropped garbage to an incinerator in the basement; an outlet for a vacuum cleaner in each room carried dust to the furnace in the basement through a pipe in the wall. The ice box in the kitchen could be opened from outside the house so it was unnecessary for the delivery man to enter the kitchen; milk could also be

The Laughlin house, Los Angeles, 1907, was a turning point in Gill's career. His changes in style followed closely his new structural systems; here he used concrete and hollow tile, furring out the walls to prevent dampness. Note the clean line of the openings.

Scripps Building and Water Tower, Scripps Institution of Oceanography, La Jolla, 1908. Gill's first work in monolithic concrete, the building was a prototype of the well-lighted factory of the thirties.

←

Wilson Acton Hotel, La Jolla, 1908, a structure of concrete over hollow tile.

Bishop's Day School, San Diego, 1909. The photograph, taken by Gill, emphasizes the sympathetic adjustment of building to site.

delivered through a slot. In the garage an automatic car washing device sprayed the car's entire surface; and a mail box flush with the front door emptied mail inside the house.

Gill summed up some of his practices in *The Craftsman*, May, 1916: "In California we have long been experimenting with the idea of producing a perfectly sanitary, labor-saving house, one where the maximum of comfort may be had with the minimum of drudgery. In the recent houses that I have built, the walls are finished flush with the casings and the line where the wall joins the flooring is slightly rounded, so that it forms one continuous piece with no place for dust to enter or to lodge, or crack for vermin of any kind to exist. There is no molding for pictures, plates or chairs, no baseboard, paneling or wainscoting to catch and hold the dust. The doors are single slabs of hand polished mahogany swung on invisible hinges or else made so that they slide into the wall. In some of the houses all windows and door frames are of steel."

His sinks were set in magnesite, which was cast in one piece with the walls, and all the corners rounded, "so not a particle of grease or dirt can lodge, or dampness collect and become unwholesome. The bath tubs are boxed and covered with magnesite up to the porcelain."

Superficially Gill might well have been classed as a rationalist, but his approach to work was that of the humanist. His passionate interest in sanitation and light was the basis for much of his simplification. His memory of his mother's inconvenient kitchen led him to devise ways to lighten the tasks in the home.

Indeed his houses were planned around women. Frederick Gutheim, architectural historian, said, "He spoke often of the practical details of housework, of the obligations of a hostess, of the house as a place for individual creative expression and activities, including gardening." In his low-cost houses he wanted a tree in every back yard so that a baby's basket could be hung from a limb.

In 1908 Gill built numerous structures of concrete and hollow tile, many without projections of any kind. Especially notable was the five-story Wilson Acton Hotel in La Jolla; the recessed balconies were the only ornament on the facade. Even these were omitted on the rear elevation. The Darst house and flats, and the

Gill used monolithic construction in the Christian Science Church, San Diego, 1909. This church replaced his smaller brick church of 1904. The dome, shown in exterior view at top right, was not designed by Gill. View through iron gate is shown at bottom right.

Waterman house used only a 2-inch projection above doors and windows. An interest in abstract design was seen in the Darst flats.

Gill liked unglazed openings in roofs. He used them in 1909, in the arcades and the sleeping porch at Gilman Hall, Bishop's School and in the shower rooms of the 1914 Scripps Community House. He even used a large opening for the jail in Oceanside, but it was later roofed over.

Nineteen eight was a decisive year for Gill; two more buildings designed that year marked the beginning of his mature style. They were the Holly Sefton Memorial Hospital for Children, San Diego, and the Scripps Institution of Oceanography, La Jolla. Both were utilitarian, with cost a major consideration. This was Gill's opportunity to experiment in concrete monolithic construction, to strip away ornament and projections and to flatten the roof.

Concrete was a material to which Gill brought great sympathy; he liked its plasticity, its durability, and its fitness for the "wholly sanitary house." Since the seventies, reinforced concrete had been employed in small buildings on the West Coast, and in 1889 it was used in the Stanford Museum in Palo Alto.

Maybeck had tried out reinforced concrete in 1907 in his Lawson house and Maurer studio in Berkeley, and then had returned to wood construction. Gill not only brought architectural convictions to the material but developed a body of detailing which made it accessible for general use.

He fashioned the steel parts to construct these buildings himself: the steel casings for doors and windows; the bull nose, a metal section that prevents corners from chipping; the steel lath. Later, fortunes were made in steel trim, but for years Gill went to the sheet metal shops to have the material broken for him from his own details. He was an inventor out of necessity. He patented nothing.

Before the hospital and the Scripps building there had been evidences of Gill's initial gropings in architecture; now he had arrived at what was dominant. In the following year, 1909, he used monolithic construction in three buildings—a Christian Science Church, Scripps Hall at Bishop's School in La Jolla, and Bishop's Day School in San Diego.

At the same time Adolf Loos, in Vienna, was preoccupied with similar matters. In 1897 he

Adolf Loos' Steiner house, Vienna, 1910, generally considered the prototype of the anti-ornament house, was built two years after Gill's first explorations in that direction.

In the Bailey vacation house, La Jolla, 1907, a dining room was opened to a terrace by two 4-foot doors on a barn door track.

The two-story living room of the Bailey house overlooked La Jolla Bay. Walls were of redwood board and battens. The room was planned around a Steinway grand piano painted red. Ernestine Schumann-Heinck and Carrie Jacobs Bond were frequent visitors.

had begun a crusade to strip ornament from buildings. In a series of newspaper articles he called down moral judgments on the Secessionists, a group of Viennese architects who had broken with the Baroque tradition but continued to use ornament. However, it is unlikely that these articles reached Gill in the small town of San Diego, although he may have heard rumors of Loos' crusade. While he was with Sullivan, Gill had learned the way the wind was blowing; he was aware of the work of Otto Wagner in Vienna, and Charles Rennie Mackintosh in Glasgow. But he could not have been influenced by the work of Loos because Loos' first opportunity to put his theories into practice did not come until 1910, with the Steiner house in Vienna. This house, whose façade curved so awkwardly into the roof, and whose stark rear elevation lacked any feeling for scale, showed Loos to be more of a polemicist than an architect. His architectural performances never quite shed the paper on which they were drawn. In contrast, Gill was first of all a builder; his forms grew out of structure. His development of cubic masses in the Holly Sefton Hospital, however, revealed a definite relation to the Cubist painters.

He expressed his beliefs in the May, 1916, issue of *The Craftsman,* "There is something very restful and satisfying to my mind in the simple cube house with creamy walls, sheer and plain, rising boldly into the sky, unrelieved by cornices or overhang of roof. . . . I like the bare honesty of these houses, the childlike frankness and chaste simplicity of them."

How did San Diego receive this reduction of the house to its simplicities? There were rumblings about "shoe box houses," but Gill's sincerity produced a feeling of trust. According to Louis Gill, he was not only interested in every aspect of the design, but had a passionate interest in saving the client's money.

Eloise Roorbach, who often wrote of his work in *The Craftsman,* told me, "People of wealth liked him for his forthrightness and honesty. His ideas had great refinement, although he often expressed them roughly. He didn't deify his work, but when he made a plan he stuck to it."

According to Lloyd Wright, "He didn't win his clients to his style by any sociological arguments, but by his great charm."

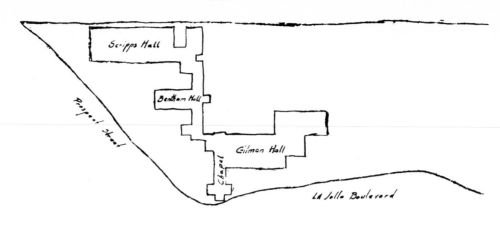

CUVIER STREET

Scripps Hall

Bentham Hall

Gilman Hall

Chapel

Prospect Street

La Jolla Boulevard

Bentham Hall, Bishop's School, La Jolla, had a steeped roof comb; similar roofs were often seen in mission architecture; the "crow-stepped" Dutch detail was used in many post-Colonial houses in Syracuse, where Gill spent his childhood.

A wing of Bentham Hall, seen through an arch in the arcade of Scripps Hall. A number of small courts were developed in the plot planning.

Gill performed an enormous service to his profession at a time when, in the West, the contractor was considered the proper person to design everything except public buildings and large residences, which were almost invariably done in revival styles. The wide acceptance of an architect in a town under 25,000 in the first decade of the century was extraordinary, and Gill deserved much of the credit. He was one of the first ten members of the American Institute of Architects in San Diego.

According to Louis J. Gill, who went to work for him in 1911, "His office was larger than any of those in Syracuse, and San Diego was then still a small town. He had six draftsmen, an outside superintendent and a secretary."

Gill was responsible for turning his nephew to architecture. In 1902, Louis, a junior in high school, worked during the summer on the construction of the Mason house. Louis's father was a building contractor; he had built two of Gill's houses in the East.

Louis Gill recalled that when he entered architectural school his "Uncle Jack" was not too approving, but asked him to study German so he could translate some articles for him. These may have been the writings of Otto Wagner, the Viennese architect whose work, according to Lloyd Wright, interested Gill.

Soon after Louis entered his uncle's drafting room, Gill made an interesting purchase. Searching for a quicker and cheaper way to handle concrete, he bought some equipment from the United States government which had been used, without great success, in the construction of tilt-slab barracks during the Spanish-American War. His first opportunity to try it out was on the Banning House in Los Angeles.

Sunset magazine described the curiosity of the neighbors as they watched men wheel barrow loads of concrete onto a huge table, tilted at a 15-degree angle by supporting jacks. On the table were rows of hollow tile—the forms for the wall. They were divided by 4-inch vertical steel bars which served for reinforcement, as well as a traffic way for the wheelbarrows in dumping the concrete. Metal frames for doors and windows were integrated into the forms. When the concrete had cured, it received a top coating of fine cement. After this step, the neighbors observed a wall, "smooth finished and complete with window and door openings, pro-

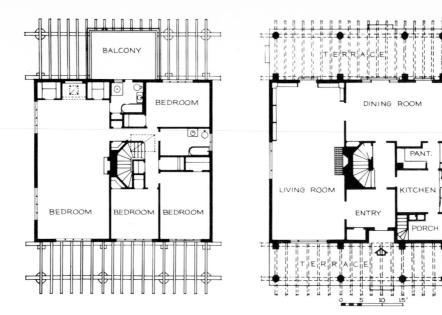

The Miltimore house, South Pasadena, 1911, incorporated into the plan what Gill called his "green rooms"—trellis structures covered with vines. He used them for entrances as well as for green-roofed patios.

The second-floor hall of the Banning house, Los Angeles, 1912, had flush paneling in the wardrobe closets. All interior halls were skylighted. This was Gill's first tilt-slab house.

Covered porch at the rear of the Milti-more house.

77

jecting window boxes and small balconies, raised to perpendicular by means of a single little donkey engine. They kept on guessing as the house took form in simple cubic units, the walls rising sheer and roofless without cornices or trim of any kind."

Gill used tilt-slab construction even more successfully in the 1913 Women's Club, La Jolla, an exquisite building with superbly planned gardens. In 1914, he—now in partnership with Louis Gill—added another building to the expanding Scripps group, the Community House for the playground, and raised walls 60 feet long.

These were low-cost structures, as were Gill's later slab-tilt houses in Los Angeles. But since the equipment often stood idle for weeks at a time, he had difficulty in finding contractors to build for him. He finally formed the Concrete Building and Investment Company, to develop the slab-tilt system for low and medium cost houses. However, it was not a success, and Gill lost heavily in the venture.

Architecture was a broad subject to Gill, it included garden and interior decoration as well as structure. From the first he was enchanted with the natural growths in the canyons, the hedges of geraniums, the windbreaks of eucalyptus, the bougainvillea burning with color on cottage roofs. Eloise Roorbach wrote in the *Architectural Record,* December, 1913, that Gill "artfully embodies the permanent principles in the straight line and circle, then starts the impermanent principle embodied in the vines and creepers, to move across the face of the buildings, graciously breaking their severity."

He worked a great deal with Kate Sessions, who had come to San Diego to teach Latin in the High School, and stayed to open a nursery on a small piece of land, now part of Balboa Park. Her 1905 planting for one of the Lee houses on Seventh Street is still almost intact. A certain unity in the planting of San Diego was due to her interest in native plants and her sturdy importations, and to Gill's constant efforts to simplify the garden.

Today some of his houses are entirely covered with the *Bignonia tweediana* which he envisioned as tracery, and the *Ficus repens* meant as embroidery now strangles many a pergola. But when a gnarled and twisted leptospermum trunk and lacey foliage is glimpsed through the

Construction photographs of the Women's Club, taken by Gill, showing his tilt-slab system. The walls were poured on platforms tilted by jacks at an angle of 15 degrees. Metal frames for windows and doors were placed in the forms; rows of hollow tile were laid to the height of the wall; between the rows of tile was 4-inch steel reinforcement.

79

Gill's interest in the total plan is best
revealed in the garden environment in
the Women's Club. His ambition to
make concrete widely acceptable was
realized to a great extent because of
the natural settings he created around
his buildings.

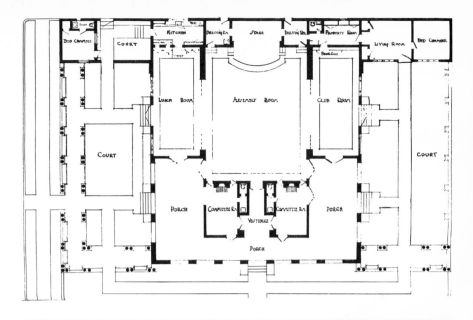

An arcaded porch of the Women's Club
led to a pergola.
←

Entrance door, Women's Club.

Gilman Hall, Bishop's School, La Jolla, 1916, was designed by Gill in association with Louis J. Gill. The hipped roof, with large opening at the ridge, covered a sleeping porch. To the right were classrooms.

clean lines of an arch in Scripps Hall at Bishop's School, Gill's ability to extend architecture into planting becomes beautifully clear.

He liked the dark glossy greens of pittosporums and the *Coprosma baueri* as screens, or as cool depths to look into from porch or terrace. The trim on his houses was invariably dark green, borrowed from his plantings. One of his favorite effects came from massing red geraniums near the house.

The geraniums, in Eloise Roorbach's words, "took a second blooming upon the walls of the rooms," because Gill had devised a paint which reflected color. What first appeared to be monotone walls were sensitive surfaces which received the impressions of all colors inside the room and of the planting near glass doors and windows. The paint was a mixture of the primary colors, added to white. By varying the proportions of the pigments, a wall could be keyed to the blues, the violets, or any color he wished.

Colored tiles in geometric Arabic patterns appeared often in his gardens. They created a rich effect and at certain hours of the day their colors danced on the walls. Living in one of Gill's houses was "like living in the heart of a shell," Eloise Roorbach said.

Although Gill's social architecture was less well-known than his other work, it was a continuing interest throughout his career.

He had built residences for most of the wealthy families in San Diego, and designed churches, schools, and public buildings—all of which were financially rewarding—but his greatest satisfaction came from poorly paid ventures in low-cost housing.

He was the first West Coast architect to give attention to company towns, barracks for laborers, housing for unemployed, and that vast segment of the population who had to be content with hand-me-downs. His favorite of all his designs was the 1910 low-cost garden court for Sierra Madre.

This phase of Gill's career began in 1908 when he built two contiguous houses on a two-acre tract he had bought for experimentation. The land, cut by canyons, appeared to be useless, but to Gill the rise and dip of the terrain added to its beauty. A single house was already on the land; he had built it for himself about four years earlier. It marked the beginning of

Community House, La Jolla, 1914.

View of Community House playground, showing supervisor's house in center foreground.

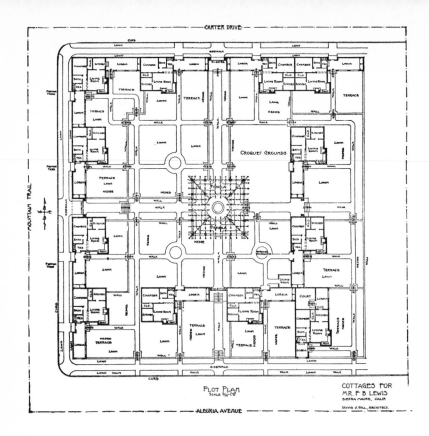

PLOT PLAN
Scale 3/32"=1'0"

COTTAGES FOR
MR. P.B. LEWIS
SIERRA MADRE, CALIF.
IRVING J. GILL, ARCHITECT.

Lewis Courts, Sierra Madre, Gill's favorite work, was built in 1910 to provide low-cost housing for working-men's families. The superb plot plan, shown here, placed the living units close to the street, and arranged them about a large open central court with a community pavilion. Roofed arcades connecting the units presented a solid wall to the street—broken only by crosswalks. Each unit had two bedrooms and its own private garden. The arcades led through arched openings to the inside gardens, and also served as living porches and entries, as shown below.

his dissatisfaction with the standard framing and plan and also reflected a simple and austere way of living. For example, in the ceiling of the main room there were hooks by which the bed was lifted during the day.

The units in his first venture in group housing were flush with the street, as was customary in the Mexican house, where there were no setback requirements. The garden wall and house wall formed a continuous surface. The front door of each house was a gate in an arch of a high walled garden. Here, for the first time, the possibilities of a variety of outdoor living spaces on a narrow canyon ledge were explored. Each house expanded through French doors to a brick terrace; one portion of the terrace was roofed, another shaded by a vine-covered pergola, and the remainder was an open garden.

The walls were mainly of 1 by 4-inch construction, but in some he used 1 by 12-inch uprights, butted together, lathed over and plastered. He also tried out Maybeck's scheme of plastering over burlap, according to Lloyd Wright.

The houses had a Mediterranean feeling: casement windows outset from the cement plastered walls and lattice work copied from iron gratings. The floors were concrete, a material which pleased Gill because of its relation to the earth floor. He had first used the concrete floor in 1894.

In the December, 1915, issue of *Sunset* Magazine, he wrote, "If half the thought and time and money had been expended on perfecting the concrete floor that has been spent on developing wood from the rough board sidewalk to fine parquetry flooring, everybody would want concrete. To overcome the popular prejudice against concrete floors is the business of the architect."

He mixed color with the cement, "usually tones of red and yellow, red and brown or yellow and brown slightly mottled. Tempered by the gray of the cement these colors produce neutral tones that are a splendid background for rugs and furniture. When quite dry the cement should be cleaned with a weak solution of ammonia and water, given two coats of Chinese nut oil to bring out the color, then finished with a filler and waxed like hardwood. Well done, this treatment gives an effect of old Spanish leather."

In 1910, when Gill designed his colony for low-income families on a square block of land in Sierra Madre, he followed the same scheme as in the 1908 houses, a continuous wall flush with the street on the north and west sides. One cottage was separated from the next by a long shallow porch intended for lounging or sleeping. On the south and east sides were cottages spaced in such a way that they did not interfere with garden areas or light and sun for the row houses.

Each unit had its own private garden, leading into a community garden, with a large pergola in the center. Less than a third of the land was used for dwellings.

There was a reverence for the individual in the plan that has never been equalled in the field of minimum housing. For years it stood as a superb example of site planning, until its meaning was changed by the construction of additional cottages in the community garden.

Gill had demonstrated that he could build a good house at a price which would allow a landlord to rent it for a nominal sum. But the court was such a success that rents were fixed beyond the means of the workmen for whom it was designed. Gill was angered by this turn of events because it thwarted his hope of benefitting the low-income groups always ignored by architecture. Gill believed that these groups had the reputation of being poor householders because no one had ever taken the trouble to design houses that would help them to be orderly. They were used to badly arranged and poorly lighted kitchens. In many of Gill's minimum houses he placed the kitchens on the front, and built drains in the concrete floors so they could be washed easily. Both kitchens and baths were skylighted, and had five coats of white paint on the walls. There was a sense of compassion at work, in plan and in detail.

In 1911, Gill persuaded the Riverside Cement Company to let him design barracks for Mexican laborers and their families. This was the first time that an industrial concern had attempted to create a green and pleasant environment for its unskilled Mexican laborers, instead of following the usual custom of throwing up shacks. Gill's sketch for the project showed two quadrangles, separated by an avenue of eucalyptus. The four outer sides of both quadrangles were continuous walls, and all rooms opened onto the garden in the center. A pergola stretched along one side.

The finished barracks are no longer in existence but photographs show that the material was clap-board siding and that instead of Gill's two quadrangles, a single one was built. However, the scheme still had the virtue of enclosing a garden, and Gill's hand could be seen in the large vine-covered pavilion in the center.

In 1913, Gill's chance to express himself fully in low-cost housing seemed on the point of fulfillment. He had just completed Echo Park Court, a series of four-room, well-lighted houses which faced an off-street garden. This was believed to be the prototype of the court system, now so entrenched in California, until Pasadena claimed an earlier one of redwood. Echo Park Court was the urban counterpart of Sierra Madre Court.

Soon after, Olmsted and Olmsted, sons of Frederick Law Olmsted, famous park planner, were commissioned to lay out the model industrial town of Torrance, to the south of Los Angeles. Frederick Law Olmsted, Jr., proposed Gill as chief architect. Pacific Electric, Union Tool and Llewelyn Iron Works had received a franchise from Dominquez Land Corporation for the use of 700 acres, near Los Angeles, on which to build shops, a civic center, a railway station and houses for their employees.

Gill was ready for a major work. By this time his planning had matured to the point where he was perfectly capable of unifying a city. His plot planning in the Scripps Group for La Jolla was a great achievement in the creation of a leisurely and logical flow of space between buildings. He had arrived at a technical mastery over concrete; he had captured the plastic feel of the material, and successfully brought his forms into a single mass. The subject of his architecture was always man, and he had the insight to plan for many as well as for one.

Gill's enthusiasm for the project was so great that he moved his office up to Los Angeles, leaving his young nephew Louis in charge in San Diego. A year went into the planning of Torrance. First to be built was Gill's bridge into the city, then the Pacific Electric Station and one office building. But of the hundreds of cottages planned, only ten were completed.

According to Fredrick Gutheim, who recalled Gill's account of the affair, "The plan had been completely accepted by management and was in the course of execution when difficulties were encountered by the opposition of labor. They objected to the plan itself, from which many traditional work details had been eliminated, because of the extreme simplicity and economy which characterized the dwellings. The climax appears to have been a public meeting in which the design of the dwellings was criticized and the architect faced a hostile and unrelenting audience."

Work on Gill's concrete houses ceased and wood houses in traditional styles were erected.

Torrance now is the major industrial city in Los Angeles County and has a population of 100,000. The Olmsted city plan was octagonal in shape with the city hall at the center; industries were placed in an outer ring. Before the city hall could be built the large site was preempted by the Los Angeles Board of Education, which agreed to operate a school in the new city on condition that the building be erected there.

Gill's graceful three-arched viaduct is now used to carry freight into the city, and the long, low station is a freight office. No trains were ever visible from the street, for the tracks were behind the station and below street level. Across from the station were two, three-story office buildings designed by Gill; they have been razed to make space for parking lots.

Gill's houses were set back over 25 feet from the street and the house walls extended to form garden walls. The off-street entrance was through an arch in the garden wall—a favorite device of Gill's which loses none of its graciousness with time.

The porches of the houses are now enclosed, rooms have been added, and the interior wall between living room and dining room removed. The skylights in the bathroom and in the interior hall are the features most appreciated by the owners. Few houses contemporary with Gill's in Torrance are still standing, and those built two decades later are already out of date.

There was one last time when Gill's talents in social architecture found an outlet. In 1933 Gutheim was instrumental in arranging to have Gill design a number of cottages for the Office of Indian Affairs as well as a chapel for the Rancho Barona Indian resettlement in Lakeside. He readily accepted the post even though he had to live on the site, design a project to be built by the relatively untrained Indians, and stay on and supervise construction.

On two other occasions Gill sought projects in low-cost housing. He made a trip to Ensenada, Baja California, in the late twenties, to try to interest officials in group dwellings for Mexican families. And just before his death in 1936, he was concerned with a project for a series of houses for the unemployed in Santa Barbara.

Up to the time of the Panama Pacific Exposition in San Diego, which opened in 1915, Gill prospered and achieved his purpose without great resistance. But his work was considered a threat to the rising school of atelier architecture in San Diego. "A dangerous kind of work," Elmer Gray, the Pasadena architect, called it in a letter to Bertram Goodhue.

Nevertheless it was assumed that the buildings of the Exposition, which was to commemorate the opening of the Panama Canal, would be in Mission style, and that Gill would be the chief architect. The chairman of the Grounds and Building Committee was George Marston, a wealthy department store owner; Gill had designed a house for him in 1904, and one for his daughter in 1906. Also on the committee was Julius Wagenheim, who had commissioned Gill, in 1904, to design a half-timbered house.

As the idea of the Exposition grew, the more grandiose it became. In 1910 Olmsted and Olmsted were commissioned to lay out the park on a site donated by George Marston. Other architects were considered for the post of chief architect, among them John Galen Howard, head of the School of Architecture at the University of California, and Myron Hunt of Los Angeles. But at the end of 1910, Gill was still favored.

Then on December 28, 1910, Bertram Goodhue wrote to Elmer Gray, the former partner of Myron Hunt, about "a position I want very much indeed, but I have just heard that it is not for me. I wasn't at first going to tell you what it is, but I think I will change my mind as follows: the post is the directing architect of the San Diego Exposition. . . . They have a perfectly lovely problem and one which Olmsted thought I was better fitted to deal with than any other architect, thanks to my studies of, and book on, Spanish Colonial architecture in Mexico. Needless to say that I am bitterly dis-

appointed at the turn affairs have taken and it is equally needless to ask you to regard this information as approximately confidential and not to take any hand in it unless you think the circumstances warrant you in so doing."

When he received the letter Gray called his former partner, Myron Hunt, who telephoned at once to San Diego. Hunt's call occurred at the moment the Building Committee was meeting. As a result Goodhue was summoned to San Diego; he arrived three weeks later prepared to design all the Exposition buildings. The people of San Diego were delighted with "such a distinguished gentleman who had made such a deep study of Spanish Colonial . . . "

Gill, with other San Diego architects, lent their services to the fair and continued to do so for a while after Goodhue took over. Gill's departure had nothing to do with Goodhue. By chance he had discovered certain graft in buying supplies for the buildings, and was so enraged that he walked out. "He could never put up with any sort of dishonesty," according to Louis Gill, who recalled similar actions on the part of Gill's stern Quaker father.

Gill would not have remained anyway, for when Goodhue was asked by the Building Committee to select a local architect as an associate, he brought out his own staff from New York instead. They took charge after Goodhue returned to his office in the East. One of his associates, Carlton Winslow, remained in California after the Exposition work was completed. In the late twenties he designed a chapel and a Spanish Renaissance tower at Bishop's School to replace a square forthright one of Gill's.

A difference of opinion arose between Goodhue and the Olmsteds over the location of the Fair buildings. The Olmsteds preferred a knoll at an edge of the park, because of its accessibility to visitors, while Goodhue, who was more interested in dramatic effects, wanted to create a Spanish-Mexican village in the center of the park. When the problem was taken to the board, the members supported Goodhue and the Olmsteds withdrew.

The effects of the Fair were almost immediate. The Churrigueresque style of the buildings, with their concentration of ornament, ushered in a period of cultivation and refinement in which there was little appreciation of Gill's austere simplicity.

Bertram Goodhue's California Building for the Pan Pacific Exposition, San Diego, 1915, introduced the Spanish Colonial style into California. The effect was immediate and far reaching; the interest created in Churrigueresque ornament turned the tide against Gill's work.

However, Goodhue did recognize Gill's importance. In a letter to Elmer Gray, dated December 29, 1914, he wrote, "I do think that he has produced some of the most thoughtful work done in the California of today, and that for the average architect his theories are far safer to follow than mine or even perhaps yours."

In 1914 Gill was commissioned to design a house in West Hollywood by Walter L. Dodge, whose fortune had come from the product, Tiz "for tired feet."

The preliminary plans were dated August 10, 1914, but the house was not finished until 1916. This was due to the extraordinary amount of detailing and, perhaps, also to the war in Europe. The building covered 6,500 square feet, and there were over 1,100 square feet of porches. Compared to the approximate rectangle of most of Gill's houses, the plan was sprawling, with a porch cutting a U into the north side and a walled court taking a corner from the south. The court, reached through the French doors of the dining room and breakfast room, served as an unroofed living area. The interweaving of inner and outer space was well suited to living needs; and the floor plan was unusually fluid.

The 300-square-foot entrance hall was one of Gill's most beautiful rooms. The walls were entirely paneled in boards of Honduras mahogany, so meticulously matched that they gave the impression of a single slab of richly patterned wood. Although, today, plywoods produced by machine methods achieve a similar effect, the character of the room lay deeper than in the fine craftsmanship or the historical importance of the flush detailing.

It was the light from the stairwell that gave the room much of its beauty. Entering through 10-foot-high windows, which filled the north wall, the light extended the upper space and determined the shape of the room. It warmed the wood to life, and emphasized the chasteness of the balustrade and the fine joinery of the handrail.

The paneling of the first floor was continued in the second-floor hall as a wainscot. Another fine detail was the hall's flush storage cabinet for linens.

The plan for the master bedroom was unusual for 1914. The bath tub, shower and toilet were placed in skylighted compartments, which could

(Text continued on page 97.)

North elevation of the Dodge house, Los Angeles, 1916, faced a sunken garden and loggia. At right was the library and beyond it, the living room. Kitchen and service quarters were at the left. This is the best preserved of all Gill's great houses today.

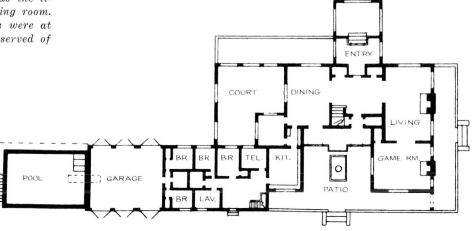

West elevation (street side), Dodge house. After this house was built the craze for baroque Spanish Colonial brought Gill's success to an end.

Hall of the Dodge house as seen from living room arch, looking toward dining room. Light entered from stairwell windows in the north wall.

Second-floor hall of the Dodge house had a mahogany storage wall. High windows in a bedroom brought south light into the hall.

The first-floor hall of the Dodge house was paneled in Honduras mahogany boards with natural finish.

Library, Dodge house.

Steel windows and door frames in the Dodge house were cast in place. The thin steel mullion had been developed by Gill in 1910.

Horatio West Court, Santa Monica, 1919, a low-cost project of four-room units on a 60-foot lot. Living rooms were placed on the second floor for a view of sea and mountains.

Christian Science Church, Coronado.

be entered from either of the two large dressing rooms. Storage cabinets and wardrobe closets filled two walls of each dressing room.

In this reinforced concrete house, Gill accomplished what he had started out to do in 1908, when he first began his study of concrete construction as an art. It was to bring concrete to the architectural importance of stone.

The Dodge house was not only a fulfillment, it was also a promise of change. The plan was freer than usual and the elevations were varied, puzzlingly so upon first encounter. The south elevation with its rhythm of arches did not predict the severe west elevation. The north side, with its deeply inset porch and the play of roof stack forms against the masses, showed a preoccupation with depth.

The plan spread out in ranch-like fashion to include a raised swimming pool and garage. The romantic gardens to the north, with their fountains and loggia, gave way on the east to propagating sheds, a corral and pergolas in wooded settings.

In the early forties, Theodore Dreiser lived across the street from the Dodge house and could often be seen strolling through the neglected grounds; his last book contains a description of a crumbling pergola overrun with vines.

What might have developed out of this new turn Gill's work was taking can only be guessed, but it seems clear that something was happening to his style. However, almost thirteen years passed before he built his next large structure. The small Horatio West Court in Santa Monica of 1919 did, however, confirm his interest in experimentation. The bands of glass on three sides of the second-story living rooms of the five-room units indicated a new concern with transparency.

In Gill's two major works in 1929—a Civic Center for Oceanside and a Christian Science church for Coronado—there was a suggestion that waiting had deprived his talents of some of their limberness.

In the small cottages for the Indian resettlement, almost his last work, he came full circle, returning to the freshness with which he saw his first adobes in California. The little Rancho Barona houses were curiously touching in their simplicity, but the simplicity was of a kind that came from a lifetime of architectural concern.

The house for Miss Ellen Scripps in La Jolla,

97

The Ellen Scripps house, La Jolla, 1916, was in Gill's final style. Built across the street from the Women's Club, the house was willed by Miss Scripps to the city, and later remodeled as a small museum. The living room and dining room looked out upon the bay.

Sketch for combination Fire and Police Station, Oceanside, 1929, Gill's last major work. Opposite is a detail of the tower.

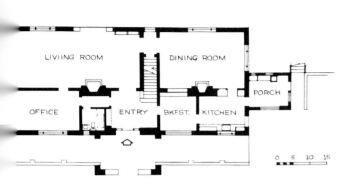

planned in 1915 and finished in 1916, followed the Dodge house chronologically. And it marked the end of Gill's classic simplicity, a style which had already been modified in the Dodge house. The Scripps house did not make any new statements in form or materials or plan. It was not experimental; rather, it summed up a period of Gill's thinking and feeling. It was bold but not imperative, tranquil but with no touch of softness.

Since the death of Miss Scripps, the house has been occupied by the La Jolla Art Center, and numerous alterations have obliterated Gill's work. This could not have been an easy task, for it requires a pneumatic drill to destroy a Gill building—and a lack of understanding of his work.

After 1916 Gill gave up his practice in San Diego. There was little work for him in Los Angeles outside of remodeling; and he was often busier with experiments than in his drafting room. One day Eloise Roorbach found him in the back yard of his Los Angeles office, on Ninth and Figueroa, working on some concrete 2″ by 4s″.

Although he was a modest man, Gill was aware of what he had accomplished, and knew that he was part of a movement to simplify structure. While his time was finding little use for him, he watched others in the United States and Europe discovering some of the essential architectural qualities he had realized, and put into practice 10 to 15 years earlier.

At the end of the twenties there was a brief respite. Gill received two commissions, the Christian Science Church for Coronado, and the Oceanside City Hall, Fire Station, and Police Station. It was while this work was in progress that he married for the first time at the age of 58. His wife was Mrs. Marion Brashears of Palos Verdes. Although he had always been enormously popular with women, he appeared to have committed himself to one woman happily enough—judging from a letter written during a brief separation just following his marriage. "My wife," he wrote, "how beautiful the word is. A word I've always wanted to use." The couple went to Palos Verdes to live, but less than ten months later he wrote in his notebook, "Moved to Carlsbad 1:50 p.m. Thursday, March 7, 1929."

The move came seven months before the market crash. In Carlsbad he lived in a house set in an acre or two of orchard belonging to his wife. It had no inside plumbing or gas for cooking and heating. Shortly after his arrival Gill had a heart attack; although he was weakened, he continued to work. He designed two schools for Oceanside in association with John Siebert. In one, a kindergarten, 1931, on Division and Center Streets, he used 18-foot openings, glazed, with French doors leading from classrooms to play terraces; this was presumably the first instance of opening the entire walls of school rooms to the garden.

Among his drawings were a city plan for Oceanside and numerous projects for Carlsbad, but it was the depression years, and few jobs were executed. By 1933 Gill had suffered a second heart attack, but he eagerly accepted the Indian resettlement project for Lakeside. According to a letter in his files from the Department of the Interior, his fee was $540.

As his health and financial situation worsened there were such entries in his notebook as: "Picked 123 pounds avacados, received checks for $26.75 from Safeway and El Cortez Hotel . . . Breakfast 40¢, dinner 60¢, cat meat 5¢, magazines 24¢."

In 1936, the year of his death, he designed a small building for Redondo Beach. His time sheet read: "Plans ordered to be drawn May 16. I. J. Gill received $20 advance. Floor plans and clerestory plans completed May 17. Elevations, sections and roof plan finished May 19. (The client) returned this date and ordered changes in plan. Details completed May 22. Work done at owner's request under full speed."

The client obligingly took Gill's tracings to the blueprinter. That was the last Gill saw of them. When he tried to collect his fee, his client's lawyer wrote indignantly that Gill "didn't build the building, he only designed it." No settlement was made before Gill's death four months later.

In a letter to his wife during his last weeks, Gill wrote, "Have been almost free from pain today. . . . It seemed mighty good to feel myself getting back into shape again. Bad luck, dear, cannot always last: so hold your strength and be ready for the good things to come. Let's help each other make the wish come true."

He died on October 7, 1936, almost forgotten, but on the West Coast which he had called "that newest white page turned for registration," Gill had already left his mark.

Loggia between Bentham and Gilman Halls had roof openings, one of Gill's favorite devices.

CHARLES SUMNER GREENE   HENRY MATHER GREENE

GREENE AND GREENE

by Randell L. Makinson

For nearly half a century the creations of Greene and Greene had stood in complete silence among the residences of Southern California. They were so integrated into the environment and topography that towns and cities have grown up beside and among them, and eventually decayed around them. Yet today many of these structures remain not only in good condition but as dominant elements on the landscape.

In 1893 Charles Sumner Greene and Henry Mather Greene began their practice in Pasadena. They were both young eclectics trained in the classical styles, but during the next ten years their work, which in the beginning had taken its form from the popular styles and wants of the clients, was directed by their own artistic vision.

The individual character of their work evolved from a rich and deep study of wood, from an appreciation for the Japanese, a respect for the Swiss, a love of nature and natural materials; and it was expressed in the bold use of heavy timbers, projecting rafters, broad sloping roof lines and overhanging eaves, extensive masonry walls, stained board and batten siding, and the incorporation of the garden into the total design.

In their twenty years of practice they established an American architecture so fresh that it spread from Pasadena to all of Southern Cali-

Stairs, Blacker house, Pasadena, 1906.

fornia and then over the entire country as the California Bungalow style.

The Greene brothers, these "pioneers and major contributors to the development of a rich and indigenous contemporary American architecture," were born fifteen months apart in Cincinnati, Ohio, Charles on October 12, 1868, and Henry on January 23, 1870. While they were still very young, their father, an accountant, decided to study medicine, and the family moved to the Mather farm in Wyandott, Virginia, where Charles and Henry spent the greater part of their childhood. Here they grew up among the beauties of nature and in an unpretentious way of life that was to influence their later work. During their early teens the family moved to St. Louis where their father set up his medical practice.

Instead of the normal high school of the day, Charles and Henry attended the Manual Training High School operated by Washington University. Each student was required to spend two hours a day at manual training, the first year on carpentry, working with and understanding the inherent nature of wood, the second on metal work, and the third on the use of tools and machinery.

In 1888 they entered the School of Architecture at Massachusetts Institute of Technology where they were trained in the classical tradition. Upon graduation, Charles was employed by the Boston architectural firm of Winslow and Weatherall, while Henry worked for a short time with Stickney and Austin, and then moved over to the offices of Shepley, Rutan, and Coolidge. It was here that he was exposed to the philosophy of Henry Hobson Richardson, whose large practice had been taken over by this firm at the time of his death in 1886.

After two years the brothers came to Pasadena to pay a short visit to their parents, but their plans for returning to Boston were soon forgotten.

California was a challenge. Charles and Henry were impressed with the bold but serene architecture of the Franciscan Missions, which lay in the quiet valleys all over the southland. And to them the people, leading a quiet life which was centered around the enjoyment of nature, were a part of the honest simplicity the Greenes found in these buildings.

The brothers' first commission, a small cot-

tage for a friend of their father's, came soon after their arrival in Pasadena, and was one of the factors which encouraged them to set up permanent practice in Southern California. Designing a tombstone was their second commission.

From 1893 to 1903 they were working under the influence of their classical background and were building residences in the styles of Queen Anne, Mission, English, and Colonial, but at the same time they were seeking a new means of expression.

In the mid-1890's, an early hint of their changing philosophy was seen in the long unbroken line of the roof continuing over the side portecochere of the Francis Swan residence. There was a simple organization of form and line in the dormer window projecting from the roof of this house that was strong and bold.

The Richardsonian influence appeared clearly in the J. M. Smith house, around 1897, where the masonry, the shingle and the arch predominated. The narrow vertical windows of the upper level beneath the roof line were the forerunners of the typical slit window, used so elegantly in the Greenes' later multi-story houses with long gable roofs. The patterns created by the groupings of these slit windows, as in the Libby house, add a play of light and establish a scale to the mass of the structure.

The gradual emergence of strong horizontals, the elimination of decoration, and the development of an over-all sense of continuity was achieved a few years later in the three-story Kenny Kendall office building by the repetition of large bands of glass windows, the strong spandrels and cornices.

The broad crisp roof lines of the L. P. Hansen house, 1901, and the clean groupings of windows, presented a sensitive but distinct contrast to the earlier Smith house.

In the James A. Culbertson residence, 1902, the Greenes brought together for the first time a number of the elements which were to become a distinctive part of their vocabulary. The house was built high on a bluff overlooking the great Arroyo river bed, from which cobblestones were taken for use in the foundation and garden walls. They found the lack of color in the gray stones disturbing so they added clinker brick which was irregular in form and offered color tones of terra cotta, warm browns, pur-

James A. Culbertson house, Pasadena, 1902. Carved redwood pergola screened the entry garden from the street.

Circular bay-window, added to the Culbertson house in 1907, displayed richly carved redwood panels and abstract pattern of leaded glass in lower casements.

ples, and black. Under the careful guidance of Charles Greene, this combination of materials became a rich part of the new architecture.

The plan of the Culbertson house took advantage of the corner site and could be entered from either of the adjacent streets. The hallway and stairwell, with entries from porches at each end, was the circulation core of the structure with the living area on one side and the kitchen, dining and service areas on the other.

While the two-story plan was compact and rectangular in form, the Greenes' early concern for outdoor living was expressed in the design of the larger porch with its open overhead shelter. Off to one side was a sitting alcove beneath a simple wooden pergola perched on two cobblestone supports. Respect for oriental architecture appeared in the detail of beams and joints and in the uses of wood and paneling. Casement windows were introduced, and in the living room were recessed into a shallow side area. This was the beginning of their later sitting or fireplace alcoves. In these windows the leaded glass was broken into an abstract pattern of horizontal and vertical lines, contrasting to the curved lines of the popular Art Nouveau forms.

Meanwhile the growing city of Pasadena was attracting more and more wealthy easterners who wished to build only simple dwellings for part-time residences. This, coupled with the depression of the mid-nineties, had created a great demand for inexpensive and unpretentious dwellings that reflected the relaxed atmosphere of life in California, and prompted the Greenes to design simple redwood cottages. These were similar to the bungalows in India, designed to house the English who desired comfortable living quarters during short terms of residence. These structures, with a shingle or composition gable roof, shingle siding, and horizontally grouped casement windows, came to be known as the California Bungalow. Their landscaping as handled in the Halsted bungalow, 1903, was modest but harmonious, with wood steps and gravel paths to give a unity to the whole design.

In 1899 Henry married Emeline Augusta Dart of Pasadena and four years later built the family home where the couple raised their four children. The house was a simple two-story structure with handsomely arranged gable roofs reflecting the grace of the nearby hills. Projecting beams of the gables made use of the

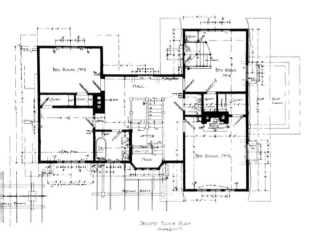

Floor plans, Culbertson house.

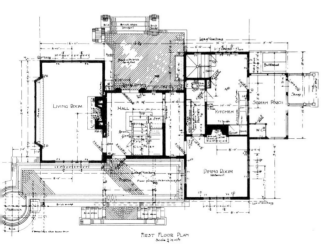

Tile detail of fireplace and wood carving by Charles Greene accented the redwood paneled walls and ceiling of the Culbertson dining room.

knee brace, which the brothers often used in the more moderate dwellings from 1898 to 1904, but which was seldom found in their work after this time. The plan of the Henry Greene house made provision for Mrs. Greene's mother and was composed of two independent living quarters, one complementing the other. Rough sand plaster, with incidental wood paneling, was used in the modest interior.

In 1901, Charles married Alice Gordon White from England, and built their home on Arroyo Drive. It was on a block where the Greenes were to build other houses, and which was later called "Little Switzerland," due to the character of the bungalows. Rooms were added as the family grew to include five children. One can follow various stages in the development of the Greenes' work through these additions. Charles' own home was a place where he could experiment with new forms and new materials. Particularly interesting were the garage doors, designed and built in 1907, with the many redwood parts put together with wooden dowels, in subtle contrast to the rugged 8-foot stone wall separating the house from the street elevation.

Charles built a studio and reading room at the third floor level where he spent much of his time, often becoming so engrossed with his work that he would miss dinner with the family. He was a little man, ill at ease in large crowds, with a nervous habit of clearing his throat, but he radiated with a verve and confidence when discussing his work. This attracted many of the more wealthy clients to the firm.

Henry was of a different temperament. He showed an immense curiosity about everything and always carried with him a small measuring tape and magnifying glass. On weekend hikes with his children they explored the hills and arroyos, and he taught them the names of the wild flowers and explained their structure; they hunted for rocks and learned the calls of the birds.

Both Charles and Henry were members of the American Institute of Architects and the Los Angeles University Club, but in addition Henry belonged to the Amphion Quartet, the Masonic Lodge, and the Americus Marching Club, a group organized to advance the cause of Republicanism.

Early in 1903 the following item appeared in the local Pasadena papers:

Messrs. Greene and Greene, architects, announce that on and after February 1, 1903, their office will be in the Grant Building, N.W. corner Fourth and Broadway, Los Angeles, rooms 722 and 723. The Pasadena office will be discontinued. Mr. Charles Sumner Greene will be found at his studio, Arroyo View Drive, Pasadena, Monday, Wednesday, and Friday afternoons.

Although their design was moving in the direction of their later work, they felt that something was still missing. They had broken from the eclectic dogma advocated by their profession but were convinced that they had not yet captured the true spirit of the rapidly growing western culture.

Hardly had they settled in their new offices when Arturo Bandini came to them with a commission for a house based on the plan of the

early adobes. The open plan principle which defined outside space proved to be the missing element they had been seeking. With the Bandini house the brothers embarked on their second and most productive phase, and within the short span of ten years they created, developed and refined their vocabulary. This was to make a real contribution to the development of American domestic architecture.

The Bandini house was composed of a string of rooms grouped around three sides of a central court. Two side wings contained the sleeping quarters while the kitchen and living-dining areas lay between. All rooms opened onto a courtyard, which was closed on the fourth side by a wooden, flower-covered pergola.

The Greenes chose redwood as the basic construction material because of its lasting quality, ease of working, and its ability to take the subtle earth-colored stains. They developed a basic wood structural system fabricated entirely on the ground and lifted into place as a finished wall. Rough board and batten exterior wall covering, and sanded redwood board and batten interior paneling, were placed before the walls were lifted into position. Wood roof trusses were built right on the site and hoisted as soon as the walls were raised. The ceiling was sheathed with the same detail as the walls. Foundations and fireplaces were built of cobblestone. Massive wood mantles were placed over the fire opening and large projecting stones formed seats on each side of the hearth.

The plan organization allowed for a free association of indoor and outdoor spaces complementary to one another, and the garden was brought realistically into the living pattern.

"One may enter almost anywhere for doors and windows are nearly alike," wrote Charles Greene in an article on "California Home Making" published in the 1905 Tournament of Roses Edition of the *Pasadena Daily News*.

There was no attempt to make the flow of interior and exterior space a single undefined area as is done today. Each space had its own identity and was related to all parts of the site development as well as to the interior. The interiors had an intimate, sheltered and darkened atmosphere, cool and comfortable as a cave, which during the day provided an escape from the hot burning rays of the sun and the dry air. During the afternoon or evening the doors and the windows—set in horizontal bands —were swung open to take full advantage of the cool breezes.

In the garden the pergola created an outdoor living room. Flowering vines became an integral part of this space, often growing over the entire structure and bursting into bloom at different seasons.

Writing of these outdoor spaces, Charles stated: "A lawn with a palm tree in the center may cover the barrenness of the dust, but suppose instead of a back yard we were to arrange an arbor leading at the side to a secluded spot sheltered but not gloomy, where one may leave one's book or work and take it up again at will."

The basic U-shape plan of the Bandini house was to grow and take on many variations. In

the Freeman Ford residence, 1904, there was a walk through a pergola, into a large central garden, around a fountain to the entry on the opposite side of the interior court. The plan of the Theodore Irwin house, 1906, completely surrounded the garden.

As the desire grew for more space in the interior garden, their plans began to spread open with the two side wings turning out from the central vestibule in a V-shape. This was seen in moderation in the Cordelia Culbertson house, 1911, and in exaggerated form in the Pratt house, 1909. An entire wall of the Pratt living room opened up to the patio, making one large living space. In the Cordelia Culbertson house the glass wall of the garden room disappeared vertically into the wall, giving free access to the outside garden. In the Crowe house, 1913, which Henry handled by himself, the narrow, long, interior court is paralleled along one wing by a gallery covered completely with a stained glass skylight.

Where there was a second floor, the rooms were related to the out of doors by means of sleeping porches. Sometimes there were as many sleeping porches as bedrooms, each sheltered by an extension of the basic roof structure. These became one of the most dominant characteristics of their work.

Broad overhanging eaves shaded porches and walls and cast deep shadows on the details of the wood joinery and shingle or board and batten clad exteriors. Heavy beams were necessary to support the long overhangs and were carried

Ground floor walls of the L. A. Robinson house, Pasadena, 1906, were brick covered with stucco. Half timber construction of second level was wood frame.

←

Theodore Irwin house, Pasadena, 1906, as seen from the north terrace of the Culbertson house. It was designed around a small interior patio.

The low sprawling Crowe residence, Pasadena, designed by Henry Greene in 1913, had an elongated U-plan with a narrower interior patio paralleling an interior gallery. The hall of the sleeping wing was widened to create a sun gallery. It paralleled an interior court and was lighted by a stained glass skylight, as shown above.

back into the heart of the house. Because of the size of the beams, the ends were rounded, tapered, and hand-shaped to bring them into an harmonious scale with the rest of the building elements. Posts were often built up of several members tied together by wrought iron straps with metal wedges which, when driven into the strap, locked the units into a fixed position.

The brothers felt strongly that wood, because of its nature, required the building up of separate parts instead of using it as a plastic material. Joints were treated as design elements and contributed to the enrichment of the whole. Thus the Greenes arranged the necessary elements with such finesse that there was little need for applied decoration or ornament.

Their reputation spread and their work began to appear in national publications. An article in *The Craftsman,* January, 1908, discussed the German character of the L. A. Robinson residence, 1906. The lower floor, entirely brick, was covered with stucco, while the upper floor was wood frame with stucco panels inserted between the half-timber structure. Such disparate elements as Japanese lanterns, hanging lights, the beamed roof, and the sleeping porch were combined into a single, unified whole.

Their work around the Pasadena area increased so much that in 1906 they established a second office in the Boston Building, Pasadena; this grew so rapidly that they soon required a whole floor. The offices in Los Angeles were later closed and all work was done in Pasadena.

The work of the two brothers was complementary. Henry conducted the business matters, ran the office, controlled the production of working drawings, and was responsible for the financial success of the operations.

Charles spent much of his time away from the office. His concern with the refinements of design left him little time to take part in the technical details of the practice. Much of his work was done in the field or in the mill operated by Peter Hall. Early each morning he went to the mill and spent from one to two hours working with the craftsmen on pieces of furniture, carved paneling, or lighting fixtures. The craftsmen recall Charles as a quick-stepping person with long hair that blew in the wind. He was not one to tolerate argument; he knew what he wanted and he got along very well with those who agreed with him.

The best preserved of all the Greenes' fine works is the David B. Gamble residence on Westmoreland Place, Pasadena. Very little has been changed since the original construction. Furniture, carpets, lighting fixtures, silverware, picture frames, linen, etc., all designed for the house by the brothers, remain in excellent condition. Here was the refined application of the sleeping porch, which became the most dramatic element of the house. No detail was left to the discretion of the carpenter; every peg, oak wedge, downspout, air vent, opening and fixture was designed into the whole. The interiors were paneled throughout in mahogany. The elaborate

David B. Gamble house, Pasadena, 1908.

stained glass detail in the lighting fixtures were designed by Charles Greene and executed by Judson Studios. Instead of the usual leaded joint, the brothers developed their own method of putting the pieces of glass together. Tiffany glass, imported stained glass, and local glass were first wrapped on all edges with copper which molded onto the surface of the glass, then the parts were soldered together. With all in place, the joints were treated with a solution of bluestone, which turned them a soft coppery green color. The effect was that of fine aged stained glass work.

(Text continued on page 125.) 113

RESIDENCE for MR. D. D. GAMBLE at PASADENA, CALIFORNIA.
GREENE and GREENE, ARCHITECTS, 215-31 BOSTON BLDG., PASADENA, CAL.
SHEET N°C.   FEB. 19th, 1908.

WEST ELEVATION.

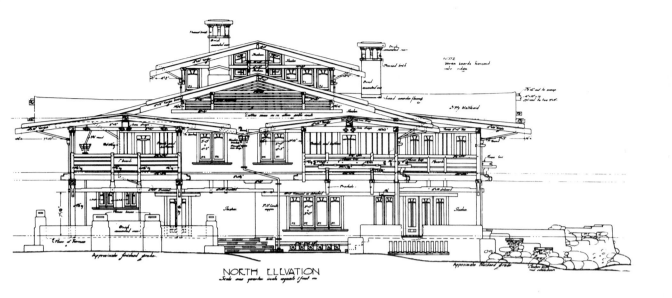

NORTH ELEVATION
Scale one quarter inch equals 1 foot 0in

Bold overlapping gabled overhangs of the Gamble house gave scale and unity to the complex design.
←

The front sleeping porch of the Gamble house sheltered a tiled terrace below. All wood was hand shaped and joints put together with wood dowels. Oak wedges were driven into joints to secure a tight fit.

Planter boxes were designed as part of the railing detail of the Gamble house sleeping porches. Recess in the splayed roof was for a large eucalyptus tree.

Steps were always handled harmoniously and subtly by the Greenes; cobblestone, clinker brick, and neatly laid terraces flowed into the plan of the Gamble house.

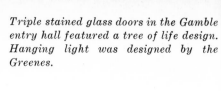

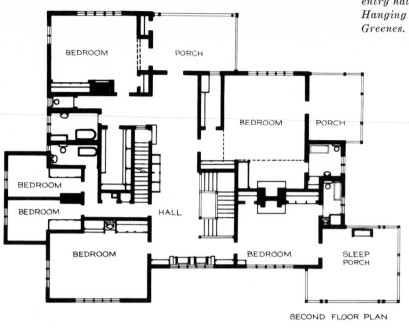

BEDROOM   PORCH

BEDROOM   PORCH

BEDROOM

BEDROOM

HALL

BEDROOM

BEDROOM   SLEEP PORCH

SECOND FLOOR PLAN

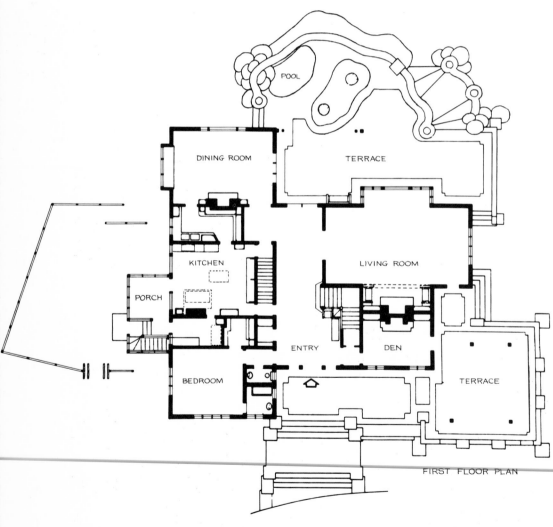

DINING ROOM

TERRACE

POOL

KITCHEN

LIVING ROOM

PORCH

ENTRY   DEN

BEDROOM

TERRACE

FIRST FLOOR PLAN

Wood of the Gamble entry hall and
stairwell was hand rubbed to a glass-
like finish to invite the touch. Rhythm
of wood pegs in stair detail was typical
of the Greenes' work.

Furniture in the Gamble house was
designed with respect for the expansion
and contraction of wood and detailed
so joints would not open. Carpet with
abstract tree of life pattern was designed by Greene and Greene.

Gamble living room and fireplace alcove with built-in seating. Lighting was an integral part of the articulated design.

Gamble house dining room. Greene and Greene furniture and built-in cabinets were detailed as a part of the over-all design of the house.

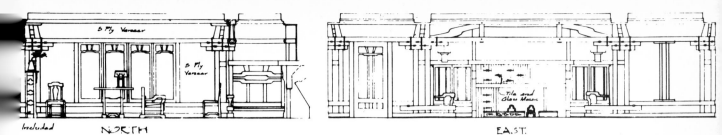

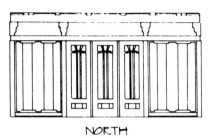
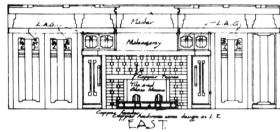

NORTH   E.A.ST.

LIVING ROOM
Scale one quarter inch equals 1 foot.
Teakwood.

NORTH

DINING ROOM.

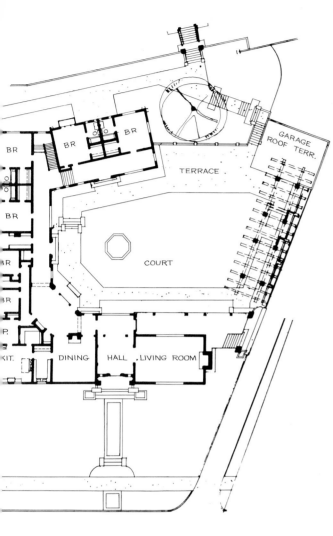

The following labels appear in the floor plan:

BR · BR · BR · BR · BR · BR

GARAGE ROOF TERR.

TERRACE

COURT

KIT. · DINING · HALL · LIVING ROOM

The Greenes captured the same rich qualities in the wrought iron railings of the Culbertson garden that they had so sensitively mastered in wood.

The sprawling U-shaped Cordelia Culbertson residence, 1911, was situated directly across the street from the Blacker estate. It was basically a wood structure covered with Gunite and capped by a tile roof, but it was designed in a plastic manner rather than in the articulated structure of wooden dwellings. Behind this seemingly modest one-story façade, two rear wings developed into a two-story structure which overlooked elaborate formal gardens below.

The Tichenor house, Long Beach, 1906, was situated on a bluff overlooking the ocean, and the pitch and design of the green tiled roof, the railings of the sun decks, the pool and bridge, and the tea house in the garden were more oriental in character than any other work of the Greenes. Clinker brick filled the spaces between the half-timber structure, and shingle was used as siding in a half-timber manner. The beams which projected from all parts of the house had rounded and carved ends.

The ocean side of the house was two stories, while the wings forming the central court were single story, with large sundecks above.

The exterior of the house is nearly intact but the dining room and stairwell are the only rooms that have not been remodeled.

The house for the San Francisco banker, William R. Thorsen, was built in Berkeley in 1908, and was one of the few L-shaped plans of the Greenes. Narrow semicircular stairs led from both sides of the property line at the front up to the sheltered entry porch. In the front wing was a two-story structure over a basement room, and this joined a three-story wing on the uphill side of the street. The enclosed yard at the back was large and open, and deep-shadowed arcades provided shelter from the hot sun. At the end of the garden were seats under a small pergola. As in the Pasadena houses, the shingle-walled and gable-roofed structure picked up the strong shadows from overhanging eaves.

There was the same refined detailing of interiors as in the work in the south. However, flush lighting was used instead of hanging fixtures, and integrated into the wood detailing of the ceiling. Large uninterrupted glass windows appeared in place of the typical horizontal bands of casements. Excellent details were the wrought iron gates and the stained glass of the front door and side panels.

Cordelia Culbertson house, Pasadena, 1911. One of the earliest uses of Gunite construction on the West Coast, its plan was basic spread U-form. Two-story side and rear wings looked down over the elaborate formal garden and pool.

Large plate glass windows took precedence over the Greenes' early casement windows in the William R. Thorsen residence, Berkeley, 1908.

The most elaborate work of the Greenes was the $100,000 house for R. R. Blacker. In the midst of rolling lawns were lotus pools set in beautiful gardens, and paths that led to and from pergolas. The character was oriental, as were parts of the interiors. The treatment of wood in the carving of the beam ends, and the subtle sculpturing of members in stair rails or lamps invited the touch of the hand. Over one hundred sheets of drawings were required to set down the construction data, and full scale drawings were made for many of the details.

Oregon pine was used for most of the structural members while the entry, living and dining rooms were each developed in a different fine wood. Light switches were carved from

R. R. Blacker house, Pasadena, 1907.

ebony and set into mahogany plates, and these, with the stained glass, had an oriental flavor.

Two wings of the house formed the small outdoor living area off the rear of the enormous entry room. To the right was the dual dining area with a glass wall that could be folded back to double the size of the dining room. The detailing of the paneling throughout was so carefully worked out that it was impossible to determine which were doors and which solid panels. No photography can do justice to the magnificence of the stairwell and entry hall.

A massive porte-cochere angled off from the entry toward the corner of the property yet in spite of its heavy structure and position it related handsomely to the design of the house.

129

(Text continued on page 138.)

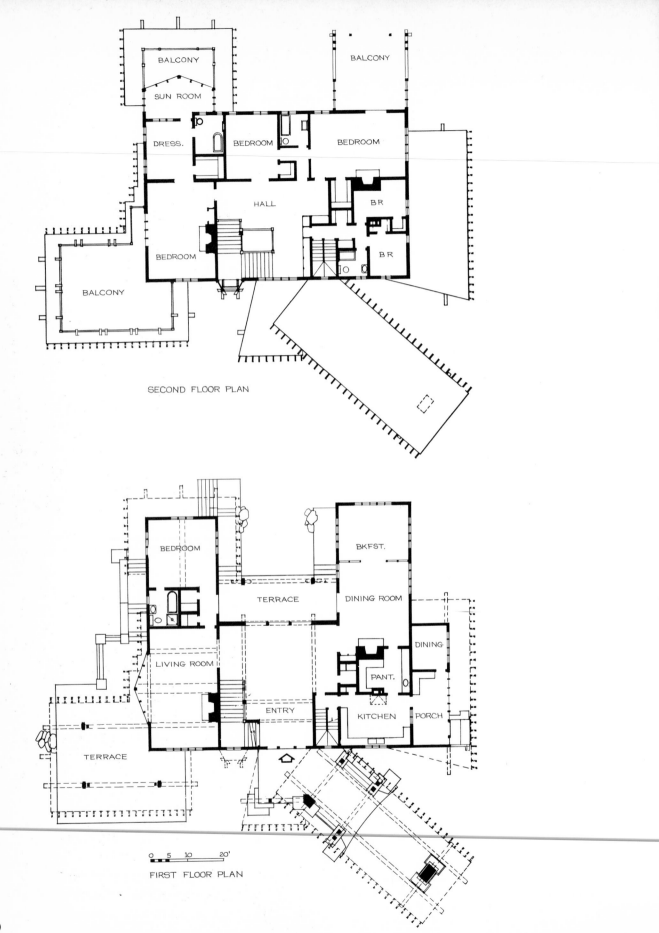

BALCONY

SUN ROOM

BALCONY

DRESS.

BEDROOM

BEDROOM

HALL

B R

BEDROOM

B R

BALCONY

SECOND FLOOR PLAN

BEDROOM

BKFST.

TERRACE

DINING ROOM

DINING

LIVING ROOM

PANT.

ENTRY

KITCHEN

PORCH

TERRACE

0 5 10   20'

FIRST FLOOR PLAN

Heavy timbers of the Blacker house porte-cochere, a bridge-like structure, were selected personally by Henry Greene on special trips to the northern lumber centers.

Iron straps and wedges were used extensively to tie heavy posts and beams together in the Blacker house; their detailing enriched the architecture.

Extensive porte-cochere angled off from the Blacker house entry toward the corner of the property. In spite of its heavy structure and placement, it related handsomely to the over-all design concept.

←

The sculptural form of buttresses added to the oriental feeling.

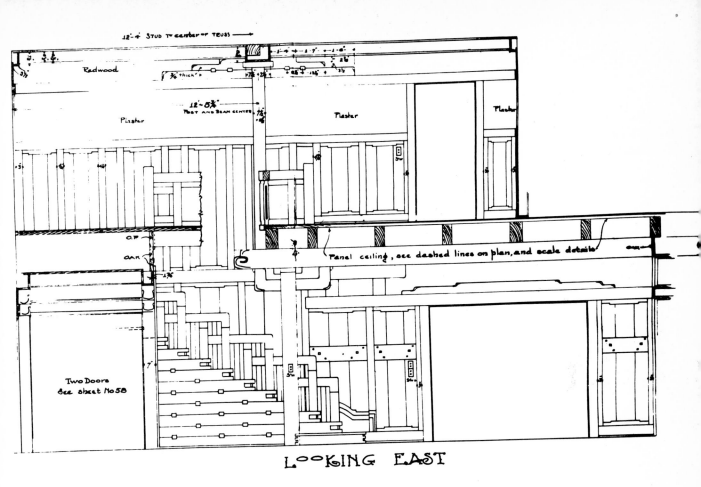

LOOKING EAST

The Greenes' belief that a wooden structure should express the identity of each contributing member was most elegantly carried out in the Blacker entry hall. Detailing of each joint was a piece of sculpture and subtle patterns were introduced by careful placement of square hardwood and ebony pegs. Light switches, also of ebony, were inset into matching mahogany plates. Wood designed lighting fixtures were suspended by polished leather straps. Deep toned stained glass in entry doors was opaque and matched the warm colors of the wood. Doors were concealed in the wall paneling and opened electronically at the touch of hidden buttons.

The lighting fixtures of the Blacker stairwell were part of the design concept and space relationship. They were suspended by polished leather straps.

←

Storage walls were concealed in the detailing of wall paneling. The second panel from left was a door leading to the maids' quarters.

←

The stained glass windows of the stairway were designed in a floral pattern. The Greenes went so far as to echo the flowers incorporated in the design into the planting scheme of the garden outside the window.

The Pratt house, 1909, with its broad roof lines which reflected the slope of the hills surrounding Ojai, was set in completely undisturbed natural surroundings. The landscaping made use of the natural growth, boulders and trees of the site. The house had a gentle curve created by the V-shaped spread-wing plan.

Unlike other Greene houses, there was no entrance hall, and the living area served as the major circulation link between the dining and kitchen wing to the right and the two-story sleeping wing to the left. The rear wall of the living room could be opened to the terrace by French doors. Broad roof decks similar to those in the Tichenor house in Long Beach served the upper rooms. Solid birch wall and ceiling paneling in the 13′ high dining room was accented by lighting fixtures, in which jade was introduced in the design of the stained glass. The furniture, inlaid with fine woods and silver, was designed by Charles Greene.

In 1914 work dropped off suddenly. The golden era of Pasadena was drawing quickly to a close. The city was changing from its earlier quiet resort atmosphere to a rapidly growing metropolis.

Meanwhile copies of the Greenes' work had for some time been appearing on the cityscape but were handled crudely and without understanding. Every builder who adapted the bungalow lost more and more of its original quality.

As tension mounted with the outbreak of World War I in Europe, the more original expressions in architecture were cast aside for the more eclectic, a trend which was given impetus by the 1915 exposition in San Diego.

At the same time Charles was becoming interested in art and philosophy. Although still just as much concerned with architecture, he needed new challenges to stimulate his creative mind. On the several occasions when work had taken the brothers to Northern California, Charles had been captivated by the coastal beauty and intellectual life of Carmel.

When D. L. James engaged Charles in 1914 to build a home on a rocky bluff overlooking the Pacific Ocean two miles below Carmel, he left Pasadena, and a year later he began gradually to withdraw from the firm and made Carmel his permanent residence. The separation was accepted as natural by each of the brothers and their close relationship continued.

Spread V-plan of the Pratt house, Ojai, 1909, formed a natural terrace and sun deck off the living room. Footings for sleeping porch, lower right, rested upon large boulders.

Beam ends of the Pratt house were
capped with copper, which in time aged
to a soft green. Entry opened directly
into living room, a pattern seldom used
by the Greenes.

Porches were screened. Open gable attic
vents provided full cross circulation of
air and kept inside temperatures down.

The James house was built entirely of stone from the immediate area and so handled that it was difficult to determine where the structure ended and the cliff began. It rose from the rocks as though a part of them. During construction Charles stood over the two stone masons and worked out much of the design right on the site. His earlier work with cobblestone and clinker had given him a background in masonry, and from this experience he developed the James house in natural stone. The arched windows and doors, the splayed walls, the chimney treatment, and the handling of detail were drawn directly from the nature of the material. The tile roof blended with stone and the development of the total mass reflected much of the adobe mission architecture which had so impressed the Greenes when they first arrived in California.

The entrance to the estate was through a single stone arch in which there was a wooden gate lighted by an old ship's lantern. A beautiful path wound slowly down to a stone paved court which led to the entry of the house. From here the turbulent waters of the Pacific could be seen through the double glazed entry and a large window opposite in the library. Trees have grown to subordinate the house which now seems a part of the site itself.

When Charles moved permanently to Carmel, he built a small cottage and studio on a sloping site a few blocks from the center of town. The simple wood frame structure was close to a duplication of the Bandini bungalow, with three wings grouped around a garden court. Materials and prefabricated structure were also similar; he planned to do the building himself. A single shed roof sloped away from the central court on three sides and, in contrast to the Bandini bungalow, there was literally no overhang as none was needed in the Carmel area.

The house was situated far back on the lot and shielded from the road by a studio of brick and tile. An arched brick wall, and a wood framed, single-car garage fronted on the street.

The studio, which was never finished, utilized the leftovers from the James house. The roof was never completely tiled. The brickwork was executed in an orderly manner and the interior had a sculptured quality developed in plaster. The street elevation was a simple gable adorned with a beautifully carved wood door in the center. On the interior was a pair of doors on

Small pieces of jade, from Mrs. Pratt's private collection, were integrated into the designs in the stained glass lighting fixtures. Opalescent glass detail was handmade to the Greenes' specifications by Judson Studios near Pasadena.

which the carving was never finished, and Charles' pencil sketches can still be seen where the carving stopped.

Charles had few commissions after this. He took a trip to Europe in the late twenties, and he spent the latter years of his life with his many friends and with his writing. In a paper entitled "Symbolism," written in 1932, he expressed his deep interest in oriental philosophy and his search for "the hidden kernel of the oneness of all that exists."

After Charles moved to Carmel, Henry carried on the Pasadena practice for some time under the original name of Greene and Greene. As world affairs became more critical, he joined the Home Guard and took an active interest in the national emergency until illness incapacitated him. His illness lasted for four years, but in the early twenties he regained his full health and returned to practice.

His largest commission was the Kelly residence near the Hollywood Greek Theatre. This white stucco structure with red tile roof was more closely related to the architecture of Gill

than to any of the Greenes' former work.

In 1925 he built the square stucco tiled-roof residence for the former Pasadena mayor, William Thum. The plan was a perfect square, and incorporated a soundproofed concrete vault, located in the center of the house.

In 1931 Henry closed the office in the Boston Building and moved his remaining practice to the family home. After his wife's death four years later, he eventually sold the house and moved in with his eldest son in Altadena, California.

Following World War II there was a renewed interest in expressing the qualities of wood. The architecture of Southern California again, as it had at the turn of the century, began to use wood as an articulated structural element. Architects became aware of the relationships between structure, materials, detail, and space, and the need for a harmonious integration of these elements into a total architectural statement.

Suddenly the works of Greene and Greene blossomed out from the shadows of the past.

Rising from the rocky cliff overlooking the Pacific, the D. L. James residence in Carmel Highlands was built of stone from the surrounding site and reflected Charles' growing interest in California mission architecture. Begun in 1917, the structure was completed in 1921.

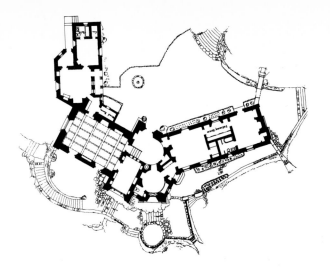

Students and architects alike realized that the current contemporary work was essentially a "Greene" revival under the rigid demands and rapid pace of an age of specialization and prefabrication.

In 1948 Charles and Henry Greene were presented with a Special Certificate of Merit by the Pasadena Chapter of the American Institute of Architects. This was the first recognition of their work since the 1922 publication of the James residence in the *Architectural Record*.

Finally in 1952 the American Institute of Architects presented the brothers with a citation in which they were called: "Formulators of a new and native architecture."

". . . your gifts have now multiplied and spread to all parts of the nation, and are recognized throughout the world, influencing and improving the design of small as well as great houses. You enriched the lives of the people. You have made California synonymous with simpler, freer, and more abundant living. You have helped shape our distinctly national architecture, and in giving tangible form to the ideals of our people, your names will be forever remembered among the creative Americans."

"In my day," said Henry in his speech of acceptance, "you could proceed to do a job and carry it out completely. We didn't need to have inspections. A craftsman's work was his reputation." He pitied those who lived and worked in what he called this period of transition.

Henry died on October 2, 1954 of pneumonia. Three years later, in June 1957, Charles died in Carmel. Thus ended a brilliant and creative era in the history of modern American architecture.

The remarks of Ralph Adams Cram, in his preface to *American Country Houses of Today*, published in 1913, are as relevant today as they were then. He says of the Greenes and the California style:

"One must see the real and revolutionary thing in its native haunts of Berkeley and Pasadena to appreciate it in all its varied charm and its striking beauty. Where it comes from heaven alone knows, but we are glad it arrived, for it gives a new zest to life, a new object for admiration. There are things in it Japanese; things that are Scandinavian; things that hint at Sikkim, Bhutan, and the fastness of Tibet, and yet it all hangs together, it is beautiful, it is contemporary, and for some reason or other it seems to fit California. Structurally it is a blessing; only too often the exigences of our assumed precedents lead us into the wide and easy road of structural duplicity, but in this sort of thing there is only an honesty that is sometimes almost brazen. It is a wooden style built woodenly, and it has the force and the integrity of Japanese architecture. Added to this is the elusive element of charm that comes only from the personality of the creator, and charm in a degree hardly matched in other modern work."

Charles Sumner Greene and Henry
Mather Greene in 1948, when accepting
the citation from the Pasadena chapter
of the American Institute of Architects.

R. M. SCHINDLER

1887-1953

The first World War brought an end to the initial phase of contemporary architecture in Los Angeles. The Greenes had given up their joint practice and Gill's work had dwindled off. There was little of interest on the scene until Frank Lloyd Wright's Hollyhock House for Miss Aline Barnsdall was started in 1920.

Wright was in Japan much of the time the house was under construction and to superintend the work he sent R. M. Schindler, a young Viennese architect who had been his assistant in the Chicago office for over two years.

When the Barnsdall house was completed, Schindler remained in the west. Under the California sun his talent matured quickly.

From his first building he spoke a language that was clear and certain. It was a cultivated language, yet never scholarly; spontaneous but under the discipline of a controlling idea; its graceful phrasing never became automatic or mechanical.

Schindler brought a particular vision to architecture, one in which materials—and even the structural systems he developed—were always incidental. He described this vision accurately in 1928 when he wrote in his notebook, "The

Entrance, Wolf house, Catalina Island, 1928.

149

sense for the perception of architecture is not the eyes—but living. Our life is its image."

His work owed nothing to the American vernacular; there was no fineness of joinery, no exquisite materials. But as William Wilson Wurster, dean of the College of Architecture of the University of California, wrote after Schindler's death, it had an "esthetic sturdiness." There was an element of surprise in his forms and details. There was movement, a variety of movement. But whatever the forms, they referred directly to living.

I went to work in his drafting room in 1944 and had the opportunity to observe his methods of work first-hand.

Schindler did not have another licensed architect in his office, then or at any other time. He employed students and recent graduates rather than seasoned draftsmen. Each night he revised the drawings on the board, and often in the morning there was a new plan in bold lines made with a blunt pencil.

My first day at work the drawings of the Medical Arts Building were being hurriedly finished for the blueprinter. Few windows were indicated in the elevations. "Just draw anything in. I'll work them out when we start building," he said. Then he leaned over the board and took a dimension from the drawing with the carpenter's tape he always carried in his pocket. He made changes in freehand at the last minute before the drawings went to the blueprinter.

During the last years his drawings became terse and fragmentary, and he designed directly with building materials as much as on paper. He took the hammer from the carpenter's hand, and the trowel from the mason's. It was the daylight rather than the drafting light that illuminated the "image."

In 32 years of professional life, almost all his buildings, except, perhaps, two or three, were executed under his direction by sub-contractors. Thus, only a limited number of jobs went through his office—no more than he could supervise personally. The financial rewards were small, the daily travel from job to job was long and tedious, but only in this way could he maintain complete control over every detail.

Schindler's office was in his house on Kings Road in West Hollywood. It had a well-used look because nothing was ever changed or replaced. He kept a row of jars filled with screws, bolts and clips on a low shelf where other architects might have stored *Sweet's Catalogs* or architectural magazines. When leaving to make his daily round of jobs, he often shook the contents of a jar into his pocket. On his door was a sign: "By Appointment Only," but it was never heeded. One day in the late forties when there were numerous jobs on the board he took the sign down, underlined the words, and replaced it.

In appearance Schindler had a curious resemblance to Rodin's bust of Balzac. He was 5 feet 7 inches in height but appeared larger because of his heavy chest and shoulders; his hair, which he preferred to cut himself, was black and bushy. He was sensitive about his short neck, and had developed the habit of holding his chin high; his photographs generally showed him with head thrown back. He had his shirts made especially for him; they were of heavy dull silk cut like a short-collared middy. He invariably wore a pencil clipped to the point of the V.

His return each evening from the round of jobs was heralded by his shepherd dog, Prince. The dog stood on his hind legs in the back of Schindler's car—his head and front paws outside the window—barking furiously at everything that moved on the sedate Kings Road.

The seats had been removed from the back of the car to make room for building materials and a bed for Prince. The door of the trunk was usually propped open by a load of lumber with a red flag on the end; there was often a sheet of plywood or two roped to the top. In the back were sheet metal parts, cans of paint and caulking compound and a complete set of tools. The tools were used to try out something on the job and to make repairs at Schindler's home and for friends. On the steering post hung a clip of scratch paper on which he wrote memos.

Schindler was fond of humor; his laughter often rang out in the drafting room with friends and clients. Whenever his neighbor, Theodore Dreiser, dropped in, explosions of laughter could be heard. They both were wildly amused by man's foibles and imperfections.

Like all the pioneers of modern architecture, there was something about Schindler's personality that mesmerized the client. He did more than inspire confidence, he created an excitement so great that clients were willing to follow him. They usually remained loyal even if the building was not wholly successful—what Gregory Ain, Los Angeles architect, called one of Schindler's "rough sketches of a wonderful and subtle idea."

Schindler might have followed slavishly in Wright's steps, for this was the most important influence in his life. He had evidently pondered this threat; while he was still in Chicago he wrote to a friend in Vienna, "Not one of Wright's men has yet found a word to say for himself."

Schindler was born in Vienna on September 5, 1887. His father was from Prague; he had come to Vienna as a child, and there became a craftsman in wood and metal. He had spent a year in New York, working at his craft before his marriage to Maria Hertl in the eighties. Upon his return to Vienna he went into the importing business. Schindler's mother, a milliner, was one of the few women awarded the Austrian Golden Cross of Merit for services to her trade.

As a child Schindler's greatest interest was in drawing. At the age of 19 he enrolled in the Imperial Technical Institute to train as an engineer. There he distinguished himself in mathematics and the statics of high buildings. Before his five-year course was completed, he enrolled in the Vienna Academy of Arts, and for two years attended both schools.

He was a student during a period when the spirit of revolt was sweeping through the arts. The revolt had begun quietly enough with the crafts movement in England in the last half of the nineteenth century. It soon spread across Europe, flowering in Belgium as Art Nouveau, and in Austria as the Secessionist movement. These groups revitalized the crafts; surfaces were cleaned up, and new sources for ornament were discovered in nature. But it was in Chicago in 1889 that a new species of architecture sprang up in the form of the steel skeleton.

Otto Wagner, director of the Vienna Academy—who exerted a strong influence upon Schindler and all his students—had abandoned his earlier Baroque style to express himself forthrightly in words and structures on the side of the Chicago school. In his Vienna Postal Savings Banks the bolts holding the marble slabs to the frame announced that it was a facing material, and called out clearly its dimensions.

As a student of painting, Schindler was also

influenced by Cezanne's concept of space, and the work of the Cubists and Futurists. They had brought space forward on the canvas, flattened it out, and introduced a multiple viewpoint. In 1912, while still a student, Schindler wrote a manifesto—later included in a collection of his papers which he had blueprinted and bound—in which he announced, "The old problems have been solved and the styles are dead. . . . The architect has finally discovered the medium of his art: SPACE. A new architectural problem has been born."

Wright found space in the Japanese print which, he wrote in his autobiography, "lies at the bottom of all this so-called modernism." Schindler found it first in Cubism; in his own work he saw *into* space.

In 1911 Schindler received his diploma in engineering and went to work as a draftsman for the architectural firm of Mayr and Mayer. He continued to study for his degree at the Academy, where his major project was a crematorium and chapel for a city of five million. Its most striking feature was a covered roof terrace; the heavy black supports, three stories high, appeared to stand free from the main structure; the general effect was of a building nestled under a high rugged trellis. The transposition of the expected scales brought a shock of surprise.

At an exhibition of the drawings of the graduating class, Schindler noticed a first-year student studying his crematorium design. It was Richard J. Neutra. He was "the first to understand exactly what I was after," Schindler told me. Both young men were oriented toward America. This was partly due to the excitement they shared over Frank Lloyd Wright, whose work they knew through the Wasmuth portfolio published in Germany in 1910. Another force, equally strong, impelling them toward America was the architect and teacher, Adolf Loos.

In the nineties Loos had spent three years in the United States working as a mason on several buildings. He was filled with respect for America's machine tools, and became the first spokesman in Europe for the machine esthetic. He also had revolutionary theories on ornament which excited the young architects. Loos wrote in *Ornament und Verbrechen,* "I have evolved the following maxim and present it to the world: the evolution of culture marches with the elimination of ornament from useful objects."

In 1913 Schindler was placed in full charge of the design and construction of the Austrian Bühnenverein, a four-story clubhouse for actors on Dorotheagasse, one of the oldest and narrowest streets in Vienna. Mayr called the project "a very complicated technical problem of construction," and said it "was handled with unusual skill."

Schindler graduated from the Academy in June, 1914. Soon after, he answered an advertisement in a Viennese architectural journal. Ottenheimer, Stern and Reichel of Chicago offered work to a well-qualified draftsman. Schindler was accepted, and Ottenheimer paid his fare to Chicago.

If Schindler had remained in Vienna until after the end of the war—as did Neutra—he would have witnessed the rise of the rationalist school of architecture. Instead he was in the idyllic land of Spring Green, Wisconsin. In the summer of 1914 the "square," which had become the signature of Frank Lloyd Wright and the modern school of design in Glasgow and Europe, was still roomy enough to include Art Nouveau, the Austrian Secessionists, and the architecture which derived from engineering and the machine.

The growth of the de Stijl group in Holland, and the Bauhaus group in Germany came after Schindler's departure. In his collected papers he called their work "an expression of the minds of a people who had lived through the first World War, clad in uniforms, housed in dugouts, forced into utmost efficiency and meager sustenance, with no thought for joy, charm, warmth."

In America there were disappointments for Schindler. He found the atmosphere of Ottenheimer, Stern and Reichel far from congenial. Ottenheimer, the senior partner, had studied at the Beaux Arts, after a brief period in Adler and Sullivan's drafting room. His practice was large, and he was prepared to design in any style.

Schindler was also disappointed to find that much of Chicago's architecture achieved its modern character in spite of itself. "What we sense to be modern in American architecture is to the American architect an expression of adverse forces, which he calls the contractor and

the budget," he wrote in his notebook after his arrival.

In his third year with Ottenheimer, Schindler designed and superintended construction on the Hampden Club and the Sullivanesque Buena Shore Club. At the same time he was drawing from live models at the Palette and Chisel Club, urging the Chicago Art Institute to establish a model exchange, turning again to sculpture, and buying a new Kodak to photograph the works of Sullivan and Wright. He also lectured at the Chicago School of Applied Art. The prospectus noted, "He believes that the creative side of architectural work is the most important, and that undue emphasis is placed on historical and technical knowledge."

In the late summer of 1915, he made a circle tour of the West. In Europe he had been a city dweller, who went to the lakes or the mountains only for holidays; he had visited northern Italy where his uncle owned a hotel. His past life gave him no clue to western cities and towns. To him they were "oversized railway stations, always provincial," and Americans were "all country dwellers who had common business houses in their cities," according to notes he made of the trip.

With his camera he recorded the Pan Pacific Expositions in San Francisco and San Diego, but it was in New Mexico that he found what he described as "the first buildings in America which have a real feeling for the ground which carries them."

The plastic character of the adobe pueblo was evident in the model he made of the first designs for the Hampden Club in 1916. The Buena Shore Club of the following year was more articulated, less plastic. It contained excellent built-in furniture, a feature that Schindler developed and refined in his later residential work.

Although Schindler expected to return to Vienna eventually—where he would probably have worked for Adolf Loos—he hoped to spend some time in Wright's drafting room before leaving. He applied to Wright for work several times but with no success. Then with the declaration of war, Schindler became an enemy alien and he was forbidden to walk over or near a bridge. A rumor that he had hidden guns in the concrete piers of the Buena Shore Club amused him, but also gave him an uncomfortable feeling. Since the future seemed so uncertain, Schindler again went to Wright and this time offered his services on any terms. Wright could not afford another draftsman but took him on without salary. The association with Wright seemed to him to be ample payment; he managed to live by turning out sketches and working drawings for friends.

On February 15, 1918, Wright moved his office and staff to Taliesin to prepare the working drawings of the Imperial Hotel. Schindler described Taliesin as a house "where free nature streams through." Living and working there made such a powerful impression on him that he decided to stay in the United States.

At Taliesin Schindler was to be put on a salary of $30 a week, with $10 deducted for room and board. However, it was not until October that Wright paid his first wages. One Sunday the Japanese architects who had been sent over to help prepare the drawings started on an outing and Schindler stayed behind. Only then did it occur to Wright that Schindler had no pocket money.

Schindler knew the financial ups and downs of Taliesin first hand. On the day the office was moved he was put in charge of the business affairs, and a checking account was opened at the Bank of Wisconsin in Spring Green in his name and Wright's. His meticulous bookkeeping described far better than words Wright's extravagances—many of which served to enrich life in Taliesin.

The Imperial Hotel had been planned before Schindler went to work for Wright, but so many changes had been made that the architecture and engineering no longer agreed. The engineering represented a year's work but "it was hopelessly muddled," Schindler told me. According to him the old foundation plan was eventually abandoned and a new one developed. A set of blueprints of the drawings Schindler made were found among his papers after his death. Wright's office had sent them to him in 1927 when Schindler's architectural license for California (he was licensed in Wisconsin in 1920) was held up until he could furnish proof that he had worked on large buildings. Ottenheimer's office also sent plans of the Buena Shore Club.

In 1919, several months after the end of the war, Schindler was again in touch with friends in Vienna. They described the city as "a tragic fall . . . a desperate milieu." Loos, still in his best years, was building nothing, and although he still lectured, it was "to a shamefully small audience," a former schoolmate of Schindler's wrote.

Word came from Neutra in Switzerland, where he was working in an architectural office, thanking Schindler "wholeheartedly for your efforts on my behalf." Throughout the war Schindler had tried to help him enter the United States.

Schindler wrote to Neutra about Wright, "His freedom is perfection. It had no tradition to overcome or prejudice to fight. His work grows quietly out of itself. He is the master of each material, and the modern machine is at the base of his form-giving."

Schindler was deeply moved by a letter he received telling of Otto Wagner's death. He was in the drafting room with Wright when he read it. "I'm glad to see you can cry," Wright told him. In later life Schindler spoke of this incident several times—it perplexed him as it might any man of feeling.

In May 1919, Schindler's salary was raised to $40 a week. In the summer of that year he married Sophie Pauline Gibling of Evanston. They lived at Taliesin and in Oak Park until December, 1920, when they went to Los Angeles, along with Wright, who was preparing to leave for Japan.

Mrs. Schindler later recalled the day of their arrival in Los Angeles. She and her husband had stood with Wright on Olive Hill, the site of the Barnsdall house. As they looked toward the mountains, their hearts sank; after the green of Wisconsin, California seemed unbearably brown.

But the brown tones brought out the shapes of the hills, and satisfied Schindler's intense interest in form; their tawniness against the blue sky provided a new combination of colors for his palette.

In an unpublished article called "Color," Schindler noted the "subtle transparent shades created by the light on the grayish backgrounds," and compared the "solid, opaque positive colors of the northern and eastern green country to the gray tones of rock and leaf" in Southern California. It took rain and dew to give the colors of the green country their fullest depth, while the sun created the iridescent bloom of the California landscape. The California house, Schindler continued, "will have to join the basic color character of its setting."

From the Pointillist painters he found the key to color plasticity. "What the poster color squares of the patchwork quilt school fail to do," he wrote, "the Pointillists achieve by joining dots of receding and advancing colors, which 'leave' the surface of the canvas and create a color world in depth. The use of a similar technique allows the architect to dramatize his space forms, change their apparent proportions, heighten their three-dimensional qualities, soften their outline, and give color to the void."

When the Barnsdall house was nearing completion, Schindler began to think of staying in California and opening his own office there. This was an important step, one that even an architect who designed in a popular style would think over well before taking.

Los Angeles then had a population of half a million, and a new boom was about to start. There were around 50 members of the American Institute of Architects in the city, most of them in the Beaux Arts system.

In the July, 1916, issue of *Architectural Record*, A. D. F. Hamlin had commented on the situation of the American architect, "The ranks are beginning to be overcrowded, undoubtedly the prospects are less certain than they used to be."

The fact that prospects are always uncertain was borne in on Schindler during the summer months by the plight of Louis Sullivan, whom he had met in Chicago. Sullivan cabled Wright in Japan for money, and Wright replied that funds would be sent to him through the Los Angeles office.

Sullivan waited. Then on September 8, 1921 he wrote Schindler, "Every day counts critically now. I suggest and urge that when money becomes available you have it transmitted to me by wire. . . . This has been a terrible summer to get through. The architects are doing nothing, and in my own particular case it has been delay, delay, delay of work expected to be authorized promptly. If things keep up lots of us will be crippled."

But there was less than $200 in the Wright-Schindler account, and Schindler, who was

Kings Road house, Hollywood, 1922, shown under construction. Four-foot tapered slabs were poured in a horizontal position and lifted into place. The joints between the slabs were filled with concrete or glass.

Kings Road house at the time of completion in 1922. Sleeping porches were added shortly after this picture was taken.

seldom paid promptly, did not have such a sum. Schindler wired Sullivan, "Will send as soon as available, ten days at most."

The following week Sullivan replied, "Since writing you I have taken in a small piece of work that I can turn out in a few days. The proceeds will help some but not much . . . the rat holes are multiplying. I learn with regret that you are financially embarrassed."

What the poet Eli Siegel called "the friendliness and everlastingness of possibility" had begun to run out for Sullivan. During the summer a letter also came from Neutra asking if Schindler could advance him the steamship fare to the United States. At the time, Schindler had not been paid any salary for three months and was forced to refuse.

That fall, while he and his wife were on a vacation in Yosemite Park, Schindler made the decision to open his own office. There in the deep woods the idea of a combined home and office began to emerge. The theme was based on one of the park camp sites, which had heavy protecting walls at the back and a light screen at the front.

When Schindler returned to Los Angeles he wrote Wright that he had decided to set up practice alone. But soon after that he and a friend, Clyde Chase, temporarily joined forces in a project to build a house for their families.

When the plans were submitted to the Building Department for a permit, word came back that it had been denied. Schindler made the first of a long series of trips to the City Hall. After hearing him out, the Building Department finally granted a temporary permit, which meant that it reserved the right to halt construction at any stage.

The house was started in 1921, with Chase acting as contractor. The two men did part of the construction work themselves so that the Schindlers could move in before the birth of their son, Mark.

The site was on Kings Road in West Hollywood, a leisurely, small suburban settlement. A block and a half away, on the opposite side of the street, was Gill's Dodge house. It represented Gill's final development in style, a classicism that was wholly western. He was 46 years old when it was built, at the peak of his creativeness but at the end of his success.

Thus today within a few hundred feet of each other, on Kings Road, are two landmarks of modern California architecture.

Both houses were built of reinforced concrete, but they had little in common. The Dodge house was a magnificent rock, while Schindler used masonry walls of 4-foot tapered panels. In constructing the Schindler house, low wooden frames and reinforcing rods were placed on the slab floor, and the concrete wall panels were poured in a horizontal position. Some of the 3-inch spaces between the wall panels were filled with concrete, others left open for glazing—"to permit light to filter through the joints."

The heart of the difference between the two men lay in Schindler's use of glass. From the first he was concerned with movement and depth rather than mass; he treated masonry as a unit through which space could flow.

"The traditional method by which structural members of the house are covered, onion-like, with layers of finishing materials is abandoned," Schindler wrote in his summary on the Kings Road house. He described the house as "a simple weave of a few structural materials which retain their natural color and texture throughout." They were gray smooth concrete; natural red-brown redwood, wirebrushed to accentuate the grain; tan insulating board with the roughness of a textile; glass; and canvas.

There was a remarkable continuity in the plan, which moved in an S-shape around the flat lot, gathering garden spaces within protecting walls and setting up barriers against the street. Exterior walls became interior walls for outdoor living rooms; the plan of the house divided the garden into three intimate areas, each with an outdoor fireplace.

Instead of the customary living room, each family had two private studios facing onto a shared garden room. Each family also had an open porch on the roof for sleeping, which Schindler called "sleeping baskets."

In the house he combined a number of architectural features which later became distinguishing marks of California modern architecture: the concrete slab level with a garden; the glass walls with sliding canvas doors to the patio; the shed roof with wide overhangs; the clerestories; the movable non-bearing partitions. The patio walls were also self-supporting screens, composed of wooden skeletons filled with glass, panels of wood, or insulating board.

The house had a heavy protecting wall at the back and a light screen at the front—like a camp site. According to Schindler, "Joining the outdoors with the indoors spatially to satisfy a new attitude toward nature and movement cannot be achieved by merely increasing the size of the conventional wall openings."

The screen wall of each studio room in the Kings Road house faced a garden space wth an outdoor fireplace.

One of three private patios in the Kings Road house, as it looks today. The concrete walls and the redwood, once natural, were painted, and wainscoting was added. Glass doors replaced the original canvas ones.

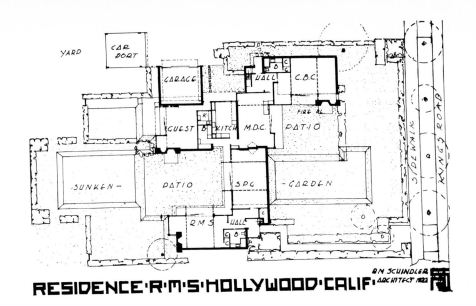

RESIDENCE·R·M·S·HOLLYWOOD·CALIF· R·M·SCHINDLER
ARCHITECT 1922

The clerestories served not only as a ventilating system, a light source, and a view opened up to the tree-tops, but were handled as a space form in movement.

Two paired redwood beams, 2 by 6 inches, which sprang from the concrete wall and cut across the studios to the patio wall, brought into intimate relation the solemnness of the masonry and the casualness of the canvas doors. The beams, 7 feet above the floor, might have been disturbing on paper but in actuality they carried a burden of design responsibility; while the clerestories raised the interior height, the beams brought down the horizon of the room and increased its spaciousness. Between the paired beams were sliding light fixtures; the space was also intended to be a pocket to receive panels for room divisions.

Because of the incongruity of canvas and concrete it might appear that the design conception began with either the concrete walls or with the canvas doors. But the two elements were gathered so successfully into one frame that it must be assumed they were conceived simultaneously.

Today the shell of the Kings Road house is intact, but it has been considerably altered. In the early thirties, when Schindler separated from his wife, the house was divided. Schindler took over the two studios to the south for his residence and office. In the rest of the house the redwood and concrete were painted, the canvas doors were replaced by glass ones, and plywood wainscoting was added in one studio. Although Schindler requested in his will that his quarters "be kept true to their origin," the redwood and concrete were later painted there also.

Throughout the twenties Schindler continued to experiment with concrete. After using tilt-slab construction in the Kings Road house, in 1923 he tried out concrete poured in movable forms for an inexpensive garden court, the 12-unit Pueblo Ribera Courts in La Jolla. A similar system had been developed in 1914 by Lloyd Wright—another pioneer of California modern design—for a hotel in Riverside.

The excellent plot plan arranged the units so that the masonry walls of one served as garden enclosure for another—a simple repetitive scheme often used today. One happy feature that has not come into widespread use, was the roof terrace. Similar to Schindler's "sleeping

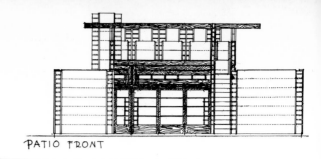

PATIO FRONT

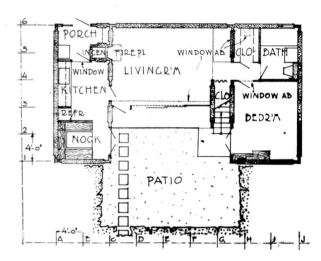

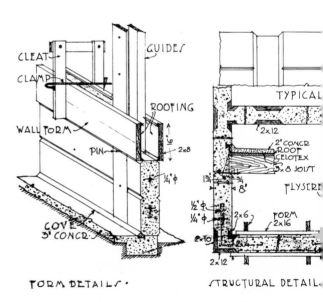

FORM DETAILS.   STRUCTURAL DETAIL

Beach cottage, Pueblo Ribera. Here, Schindler used what he called "slab-cast construction," in which concrete was poured into movable forms. No attempt was made to conceal the horizontal form marks.

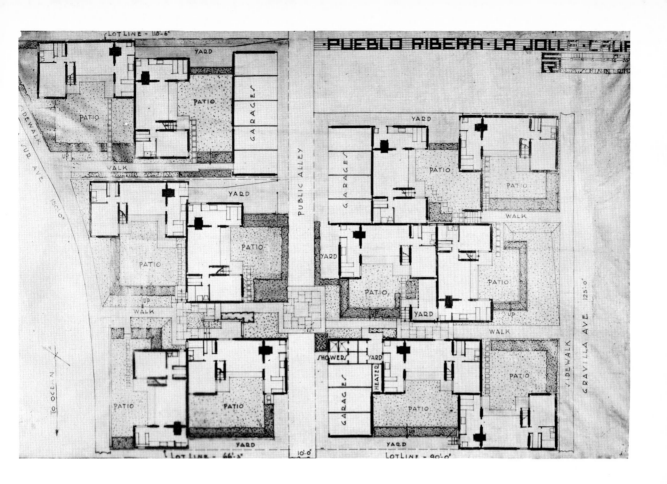

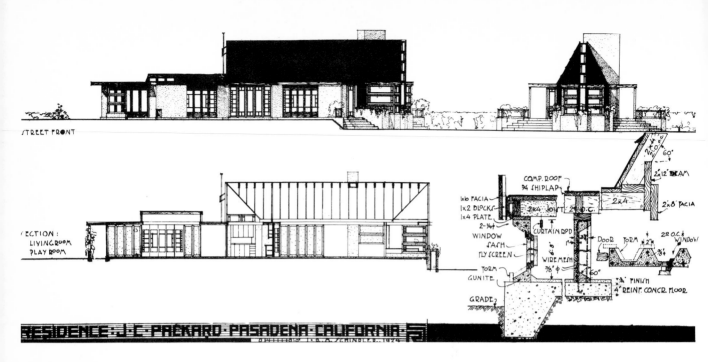

STREET FRONT

SECTION:
LIVING ROOM
PLAY ROOM

COMP. ROOF
¾ SHIPLAP
1x6 FACIA
1x2 BLOCKS
1x4 PLATE
2-¼Ø
WINDOW
SASH
FLY SCREEN
FORM
GUNITE
GRADE
2x12 BEAM
2x4
2x8 FACIA
2x4   JOIST 2 O.C.
CURTAIN R'D
DOOR   FORM   2"
WIRE MESH
⅜ Ø
FINISH
4" REINF. CONCR. FLOOR
2 O.C.
WINDOW

RESIDENCE : J. C. PACKARD PASADENA CALIFORNIA
R. M. SCHINDLER. 1924

baskets," it offered each tenant a sitting room with an unobstructed view of the sea.

Schindler did not approach a minimum house from the point of view of how much could be left out; he exercised the strictest economy on structure so that he could indulge in what he considered the vital luxuries of life. Here the luxuries were three different types of living areas: indoors, enclosed court and roof terrace, each communicating naturally with the others.

In the lift-form concrete system he achieved an organic whole out of an aggregation of small units. The form work was both ingenious and simple. After the concrete floors were poured, vertical guides were erected; then window and door frames were introduced, and plumbing pipes and reinforcing rods placed between the forms. One course of concrete was poured each afternoon; the following morning the forms were lifted along the vertical guides and locked into place ready for pouring another course. Only two sets of forms were used for the 12 units.

Like Gill, Schindler was impatient with the standard balloon frame. He objected to the use of studs over a wooden skeleton, describing it in his notes as "an inorganic, unelastic plaster slab supported by means of an organic swelling and shrinking skeleton."

For the 1924 Packard house in Pasadena, he experimented with Gunite for thin self-supporting exterior walls, with reinforced concrete studs integral with the slab floor. Here Schindler came up against an "art jury," a committee of laymen who passed on the architectural design. Such committees were widespread at the time and the modern architect was forced to abide by their arbitrary rulings. One of the requirements for the Packard house was a pitched roof. Schindler extended his thin concrete walls up to standard door height and then treated the entire upper structure as a roof. Deep mitres were cut in the gable ends, and the south roof was opened with glass. He had abided by the letter of the law if not the spirit. The Y-shaped plan of the house, embracing a garden, was more successful than the form.

Schindler made another novel use of concrete in 1926 in the Lovell vacation house at Newport Beach. This was the third house he had designed for Dr. Lovell; the first, in 1924, was a mountain cabin in which shop-fabricated panel walls

For the Packard house, Pasadena, 1924, Schindler used "slab-gun construction." In this system Gunite was blown from a gun against upright panel forms to produce both concrete walls and reinforced concrete studs in one operation.

163

In the Lovell beach house, Newport Beach, 1926, living space was developed inside of five free-standing reinforced concrete frames, cast in the form of square figure eights. Schindler objected to pipe column stilts, calling his own system "projections of five visible concrete frames which form an organic skeleton."

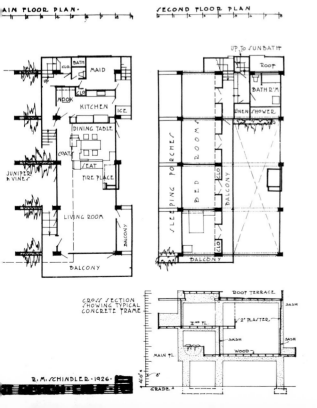

were installed; the second, in 1925, was a concrete block house for a Fallbrook ranch.

In the beach house Schindler developed living space inside five free-standing concrete frames cast in the form of square figure eights. Two-inch-thick solid plaster walls and pre-milled units containing window and door openings were hung by steel rods from the free-standing concrete frames.

A balcony off the two-story living room led to the bedrooms; these in turn led through French doors to a sleeping porch running the length of the house. Some years later the Lovells wanted the porch enclosed. Schindler, who always took charge of even the smallest repairs on his buildings, instructed the carpenter to remove the French doors and install them above the porch rail to make the enclosure.

The Lovell house was not primarily a drawing board solution—as was much of the work done at that time by the Constructivists in Europe. Schindler's purpose in using the frames was to raise the house above the public beach, and also to develop a skeletal system solid and flexible enough to withstand earthquakes. Five years later a series of earthquakes which destroyed a school several hundred yards away, merely rocked the Lovell walls in their concrete cradles.

While the Lovell house was on the board, Neutra and his wife and son came to live in one of the studio rooms in the Kings Road house, and Neutra started his own practice in Schindler's drafting room. One of their two joint projects was a civic center for Richmond—in collaboration with the city planner Carol Aronovici. The work was not executed. Another joint project was a design for the League of Nations competition, a building also hung from a series of concrete frames. The first prize went to Le Corbusier, but the Schindler-Neutra entry received an award.

Neutra's commission to do a town house for Lovell—Schindler's best client—gave Neutra an opportunity to establish his own office. However, it was inevitable that the Neutra-Schindler association should end because of the conflict in their approach to design.

The Lovells and the Sam Freemans, Mrs. Lovell's sister and brother-in-law, were staunch patrons of the new architecture in the Los Angeles area. During the twenties they braved

In the Sachs apartment house, Los Angeles, 1928, Schindler turned from concrete to studs and plaster—his first attempt to develop his own vocabulary within standard framing. Each apartment had an entrance from the street and a glass wall facing a living porch.

public opinion and loan agencies (none of the houses was mortgageable) to commission Schindler, Neutra and Wright to design houses for them.

It was during this period that Schindler's friendship with Wright was broken. Wright apparently had not quite forgiven Schindler for establishing his own office, and in several letters —all signed "Affectionately"—he made references to Schindler's lack of loyalty. Schindler accepted the gibes philosophically because of his great affection for Wright. In 1931 an exhibition of the work of Wright, Neutra, Schindler, J. R. Davidson, Kem Weber and Jacques Peters was arranged. Wright was angered by the catalogue, which stated that Schindler had been in charge of his office during Wright's stay in Japan, and asked that his work be removed from the exhibit. He also wrote Schindler a letter denying that he had ever left anyone in charge of his office, and calling Schindler a green apprentice and a draft dodger whom he had befriended.

Schindler replied with such ferocity that no further relationship between the two men was possible. "The structural features which hold the Imperial Hotel together," he wrote, "were incorporated only after overcoming your strenuous resistance." He listed seven jobs that had been started after Wright's departure and drawn without his "presence and help." He continued, " You were informed of all this work by letters and blueprints I sent to Japan. You accepted it and paid for it (as little as you could). You officially identified yourself with it by including my scheme and drawing of Mr. Hardy's workingman's colony unretouched in your personal exhibit as your own."

Schindler never saw Wright again. Ten years later Wright came one day to Kings Road while Schindler was away, but Schindler made no effort to get in touch with him. The chapter with Wright was closed; it could never be reopened. Schindler buried his disappointments. "We ourselves are the keepers of our feelings," he wrote in his notebook in 1927. "It is up to us to handle them quietly."

Schindler had made an uncannily correct autobiographical statement in the design of his Kings Road combined residence and office— with its guarding masonry front and its charming intimate views of gardens. His explosive laughter and his charm could not quite hide the recluse who reserved himself almost wholly for himself.

Following the Lovell beach house, Schindler began to lose interest in techniques and settled down to an exploitation of forms. In 1928 he wrote in his notebook, "Tecknik = type based on human laws. Art = variation seen through a human mind." In an apartment house of studs and plaster, designed that year for Herman Sachs, he made poetic use of standard materials.

The apartment house was remarkable in that there was no long central hall; each apartment was oriented toward a private living porch. Today there is a long waiting list for the apartments.

Much of Schindler's exuberance found its way into his designs; a particularly happy example is the 1929 Wolfe house on Catalina Island. The lot was only 30 by 40 feet, and in some places the grade was as steep as 45 degrees. Schindler was a master at hillside planning, and the Wolfe house was the first test of his abilities in this field.

At that time most hillside houses were designed as part of the slope, and an enormous amount of excavation was required for foundations and retaining walls. In Schindler's notes on the Wolfe house he wrote that he had consciously abandoned "the conventional conception of a house as a carved mass of honeycombed material protruding from the hillside, and created a composition of space units to float above the hill."

The house rode above the slope, and appeared to have the weight of a butterfly. Only the foliage from the abundance of flower boxes laced it back into the slope. To emphasize lightness, all vertical members were suppressed. Schindler planned the house to the setback lines on all sides, kept the openings small on the street front and toward the neighbors but glazed the entire downhill side toward the view—Catalina Bay to the south and the ocean to the east. As there was no space for outdoor living, he developed a garden environment in a series of deck terraces. A ramp connected the living room level and the roof terrace.

His interest in concrete was not entirely forgotten; he used a thin sandwich of concrete and corrugated iron to form waterproof floors and terraces. The roof ceilings were treated as one element—a prediction of his later use of tongue-and-grooved planking for ceilings and a base for roofing paper.

One of the practices Schindler initiated here, and later repeated many times, was to place the master bedroom several feet above the living room. Sliding wall-panels opened the two rooms. The bedroom ceiling was high enough to allow space for a strip of clerestory windows. They admitted the morning sun and in summer, a cooling airstream that lowered the temperature of the roof.

By 1930, when the depression began to be felt, Schindler had executed a surprisingly large amount of work—in view of the fact that modern architecture was still unacceptable to the general public. There were 11 residences, three apartment houses, three courts, two cabins, six shops and a private school, as well as two additions, a loggia and pond, for the Barnsdall house. (An addition for the Helena Rubinstein house in Greenwich, Connecticut took him to the East in 1923. This was his only trip away from the West Coast after he established practice there.)

Styles in domestic architecture had gone through several changes. Spanish Colonial, introduced through the 1915 San Diego Pan Pacific Exposition, had soon given way to Spanish and Italian styles; these fell of their own weight, and were followed by the revival of a style indigenous to California. It was based upon the thick adobe walls and Colonial woodwork which had developed around Monterey in Northern California. By 1931 the Monterey work yielded to the Colonial style of the middle Atlantic states and to the late Georgian.

As one revival style succeeded another, Schindler was evolving his own personal approach to architecture, based on an ideal of living. He was a persuasive spokesman for modern architecture, and carried on his own educational campaign. Whenever a loan agency refused to finance one of his buildings, he called on its directors to explain his purpose in breaking with tradition. He even addressed a group of escrow officers on the principles of modern architecture.

He simplified his plans and detailing so they could be easily understood by the building trades, upon whom the modern architect depended to carry out his ideas. He realized that

168

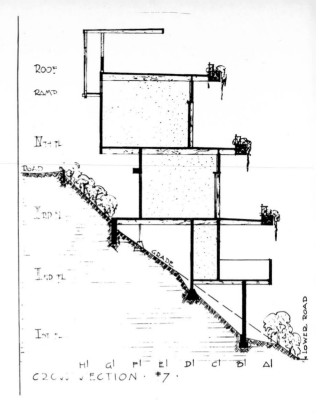

Wolfe house, Catalina Island, 1928. A masterpiece of hillside planning on a small steeply sloping site, it covered most of the 30 by 40-foot area. The house was planned to the setback lines, with no gardens. Each floor received extensive terraces to provide outdoor living spaces. The roof, designed for play activities, was reached by a ramp from the living room which had a view of Catalina Bay to the south. The sliding glass doors joined the living room and deck terrace.

William Oliver house, Los Angeles, 1933. Built on a hillside lot, the house had a wood stud frame which was modified to permit a wider use of large glass areas. It was built at a cost of $4 per square foot. The living room was furnished with Schindler's unit furniture, which could be assembled in a variety of combinations. Schindler felt that furniture should merge with the house, leaving the room free to express its form.

perspective drawings and sectional views were of little value in describing his buildings. "To visualize a space form," he wrote in his notes, "one must be inside it."

He used 4-foot grid lines on his working drawings, the lines keyed to numbers and letters. His plans specified that battens be placed in a continuous belt around a building under construction; numbers and letters of the unit lines were transfered to the batten and a nail was set at each location. By referring to the plans, the carpenter could readily find any portion of the building.

The unit lines were also an aid to Schindler in dealing freely and accurately with complicated forms; he found that the larger unit of measurement helped in giving his structures scale, rhythm, and cohesion. When making his decisions relating to size values mathematical computations were unnecessary.

In an article, "Reference Frames in Space," *Architect and Engineer*, April 1946, Schindler stated that it was impossible "to maintain an interlacing rhythmic play on a plan which indicates dimensions in figures," and that he regarded measurements in numbers as "abstractions devoid of human connotations." He believed that the metric system was unrelated to human beings and was of value mainly to engineers.

His frame of reference was the 4-foot module, which did not cramp his freedom of design and related well to the human scale. He felt that this module established good proportions as a rule. Schindler, according to his article, viewed proportion as "a live and expressive tool in the hands of the modern architect who uses its variations freely, to give each building its own individual feeling."

Early in the thirties, Schindler abandoned skeleton design in which interior spaces were determined by the frame. He preferred to work entirely in skin design, where it was possible to organize forms irrespective of structure.

He made his peace with the standard wood frame, but on his own terms. It was through freedom of structure, he felt, that modern architecture would achieve what the past called "style."

Instead of using the typical double-plate line at the 8-foot level, he set the plate course at door height, and all studs were cut to that dimension. This made it unnecessary to cut into his plate line each time there was a variation of ceiling height. Door and window frames were placed either below or above the plate. Walls were raised to the required height by use of a band of clerestories, which rested on the top plate course.

Working with studs and plaster he was able to build at a cost low enough to compete with the contractor's house. He had always been concerned about the overindebtedness of the homeowner, who paid double the price of a house before it was debt-free and got a poor product in the bargain.

He saw the absurdity of looking for structural short-cuts to save a few dollars when the cost would be doubled by the loan anyway, but he explored all the possibilities. In 1933, he designed a 600-square-foot concrete shell with shop-fabricated, movable wardrobe closets, which could be placed in various positions to divide the floor space. In 1935, he designed elements for a prefabricated house which could be adjusted to any plan. The structural system was panel-post; and 4-foot panels of glass, plywood, plastic or other materials were inserted between posts.

His minimum houses of the thirties ran from $3.50 to $4.00 a square foot. They had such features as glass-walled patios, good transitions from entrance hall to living room, and bathrooms with Pullman basins. There were also clerestories to admit light where it was least expected, desks tucked away into space that might have been wasted, and a great variety of well-planned storage cabinets. These features would have made any house distinctive; but in Schindler's development of good living spaces, the spontaneous play of one form against another made some of his houses small masterpieces. The 1933 Oliver house was one example.

It was built at a cost of $6,400 and covered an area of 1600 square feet. The forms were concentrated but, as the observer moved around them, they dissolved and reappeared in new contexts. The inner space seemed to flow through and around the outer space. In the living room some of the Schindler unit furniture, developed in 1931, served as unifying elements.

When designing the units, he had tried to

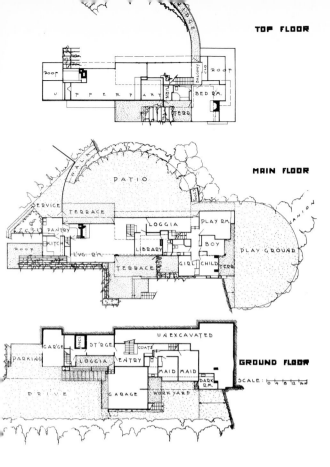

PATIO

SERVICE TERRACE
PANTRY
LOGGIA PLAY RM.
KITCH LIBRARY BOY
LIV'G RM.
TERRACE GIRL CHILD TERR
PLAY GROUND

ROOF UPPER PART BALCONY CLO ROOF
BED RM.
TERR

GARAGE STORGE COATS UNEXCAVATED
PARKING LOGGIA ENTRY
MAID MAID
DRIVE GARAGE WORK YARD DARK RM.

SCALE:

West elevation, Rodakiewicz house, Beverly Hills, 1937. This fourteen-room, three-story hillside house was Schindler's most ambitious work in imaginative cubism.

In the Buck house, Los Angeles, 1934, Schindler developed harmonious balance and counter balance.

achieve forms that did not become furniture shapes when placed against a wall. They were low and wide and could be combined to create various pieces of furniture; he thought of them as "floor terraces" rather than furniture. Fine woods were used, and the cabinet work was excellent. Before developing the unit furniture, Schindler had designed various small stools, tables and sideboards, on the job, from leftover scraps of wood. These had great charm and spontaneity and were so satisfactory that they are still in use in many of his early houses.

The Oliver house and the 1934 Buck house were reminders of the theories of the Futurist painters. Their 1910 manifesto, concerning the successive stages of an object in motion, the projection of force lines, simultaneity, and the interpenetration of planes, might have been written for architecture, as well as for painting.

The deliberate movement of forms from east to west on the street elevation of the Buck house seemed to echo a phrase in the Futurist manifesto, "Only by means of motion does the object enact its drama. . . ."

During the thirties the Silverlake district in Los Angeles became a center for Neutra and Schindler houses. Schindler built six large hillside houses there for various clients, including Droste, the Dutch consul in Los Angeles. Built of wood frame and stucco, the houses were reminiscent of the Cubist school of painting. At that time, the work of the Dutch Constructivists and Lurçat of France was appearing in Europe but its two-dimensional aspect had little interest for Schindler in his search for depth of form. He had lost touch with all his old friends in Europe; his design developed naturally out of his own deep architectural concerns, which were rooted in California.

Almost the last of Schindler's work in imaginative Cubism was the 1937 Henwar Rodakiewicz house. Here he achieved such fluidity that no line had beginning or end. Low, thin parapet walls gave an upward swing to wide stucco-covered overhangs, and small wall fins added a counter motion; these lines were tributary to others, until the whole was a lyrical interplay of forms. Nothing was tied down—this was one of his design principles. "Once an architect begins to worry about tying things down and about correct spacings," Schindler told his draftsmen, "he arrives only at formal harmonies, and

Gisela Bennati cabin, Lake Arrowhead, 1934. An A-frame on a sloping pine-covered lot, the six-room mountain cabin was wood frame and plywood on a local stone base. The gable ends were of glass.

←

→

Corner of Bennati cabin living room. The glass gable looked out over wooded slopes. Plywood was used between the 4 by 6-inch rafters, 4 feet on center.

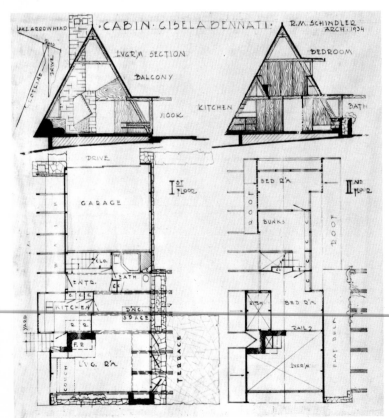

Schindler flattened out the 60 degree roof pitch for terrace doors and continued the roof beams inside the shell. A bedroom was on the balcony above the living room.

these have little to do with living."

The 1934 Bennati cabin, the first of the A-frames in architecture, had a spontaneity that made the later A-frames seem over-studied. Its form grew out of the restrictions for the tract at Lake Arrowhead; all cabins were required to be in Norman style. Schindler, tongue-in-cheek, designed the roof to the ground. When the business men on the art jury expressed doubt that the design was pure Norman, Schindler gathered up a sheaf of old fox-marked prints of steep-roofed houses. He laid them in the laps of the jury and said, "Don't you recognize these, gentlemen? Pure Norman!" No one on the jury had been to Normandy so the design was passed.

The employment of local stone and the poetic use of the sloping site gave the house something of an indigenous character among the borrowed forms of the other houses. Fir plywood was used between the framing members for walls and cabinets. Schindler was quite at home with this new industrial material. Six rooms were contained within the all-roof cabin, with bedrooms off a balcony.

Schindler lost his battle with Mrs. Bennati to select the colors. As an art teacher she considered this her province, while Schindler maintained that color was an architectural element. He wasn't used to defeat, and actually was sick over the incident, according to Mrs. Bennati.

None of Schindler's cabins had a trace of rusticity. He was an urbanite, and this was always reflected in his style. His small city houses had no air of the cottage about them; he gave them an informal dignity that did much to lift Los Angeles out of a prolonged provincialism.

He made few contributions to landscaping, for his interest in the garden stopped with the terrace. He worked extraordinarily well with what he found on the site; his integration of trees into the architectural scheme showed love and respect for them. However, unlike the Greenes and Gill, he did not develop total gardens as part of the architecture. (He never at any time had budgets comparable to the Greenes'.)

The Greenes and Gill also far outstripped Schindler in the planning of the kitchen, a room to which he gave only perfunctory attention. His built-in tables were awkward, and the space arrangement often poor. His approach to the

Dekker house, Woodland Hills, 1940. In this beautiful example of site planning, the rhythm of roof lines echoed the roll of the hills. The green of sheet copper roofing blended with the dusty green of live oaks.

kitchen was that of a Viennese bachelor who was accustomed to servants. He gave far more attention to the bathroom, where he achieved real elegance with built-in dressing tables and cabinets, and excellent lighting from clerestories. The bathrooms were seldom rectangular, but borrowed space from adjoining rooms to create the luxury of ampleness.

In all his houses of the thirties, Schindler established good practices in the use of glass. His notes indicate that he saw the ability of light to define space as an "invaluable tool to the designer who is able to create space forms without solid partitions." And in his compositions, he treated glass as light.

Glass was never used for a picturesque effect, nor did it ever violate the privacy of a room. Large glass areas were always protected with wide overhangs and faced closed gardens or distant views. Schindler avoided large windows that might transform a room into a cave and "force the occupants to face a glaring light source at all times."

He extended glass to the floor only after examining all of the disadvantages, and usually preferred a single glass door to large, sliding glass ones. He developed a great variety of windows. Like Maybeck, he saw the advantage of the pivoted awning-type window, which he often used in strips to ventilate rooms in the hot San Fernando Valley.

He had an astonishing inventiveness and developed dozens of new parts for every house. He designed the hardware and the sheet metal parts for sliding windows and doors. The flush ceiling lighting and cove lighting in the Buck house were fabricated from his designs. His dislike of shiny hardware "which places an object out of reach of a close personal relationship," led him in 1926 to invent undercut grooves to take the place of drawer pulls. He considered a shiny knob "as objectionable as an actual hole in the material." All shiny surfaces were to him a "negation of texture." (The quotations in these paragraphs are from Schindler's notes on reflectors.)

Changes in Schindler's style were apparent by 1940. In the last phase of his work there was a wider use of wood and greater emphasis on the roof. A transitional work was the 1938, combination music studio and home for Mrs.

Mildred Southall. The plywood which formed

Southall house, Los Angeles, 1938. One of the first all-plywood houses, it had 4 by 4-foot awning-type windows. The living room was planned as a children's classroom for the study of music. The seat below the bookcase was a storage cabinet for classroom equipment. The adjoining bedroom shared the living room view through sliding panels. A typical practice of Schindler's was to raise the bedroom above the living room level so the view was unobstructed by furniture.

an interior and exterior skin was treated with remarkable sympathy. This product of industry had great pliancy in Schindler's hands and was applied with considerable frankness. His use of plywood was indicative of his good practices with other new materials, especially corrugated plastic, which he used, in 1950, for the roof of the Tischler house and for the exterior walls of the Janson house.

The full transition from the old to the new came in the 1940 house for Albert Dekker. Up until this time Schindler's roofs had been almost flat. But in the Dekker house the pitches and counter movement of the roofs on the various levels reflected the rise and drop of the surrounding hills. The change was emphasized by the sheet copper roofing material, which seemed singularly at home among the live oaks growing in the creases of a knoll on the site.

By 1944, when I went into his office, Schindler "looked for the roof" as he drew the floor plan; and he placed his clerestories above the areas where he wanted daylight to enter. I recall how he spun the arms of the drafting machine as he searched for a roof of a house designed on a system of 30-60 degree angles.

That was the first time he designed with a drafting machine. When I first brought my drafting machine into the office, it made him uncomfortable; he claimed that it was inaccurate. Each night he revised drawings; in the morning the machine was invariably pushed to the top of the board and the T-square rested on the tracing paper.

At that time the Bethlehem Baptist Church was under construction; the pulpit and pews were being designed. Construction was ready to start on the Medical Arts Building, and there were four houses in various stages of design. Soon a second draftsman was employed, and when he also turned up with a drafting machine, Schindler gave us a little lecture. The gist of it was that one could never get the feel of architecture by using a machine. He told us we could keep the machines in the office—if we were so foolish—as long as we got them out of his way each evening. Then one Monday morning about a month later I discovered Schindler sitting at my drafting board whirling the arms of the machine with great dexterity. He seemed to be enjoying himself immensely.

"When did you learn to use it?" I asked in

Bethlehem Baptist Church, Los Angeles, 1944. The arcade and grounds were planned for outdoor social functions. The stairs led to an open air theatre. Schindler made the tower an element in the interior design by glazing the interspaces of the cross form in the roof. Receding courses of stucco walls closed out the sound and sight of heavy traffic on the busy street. With no attempt to imitate masonry, Schindler achieved a sense of massiveness through the width of the courses and the shadow line.

astonishment. "It requires no special knowledge," he said.

His T-square never again appeared on the drafting board. It was typical of Schindler to keep any machine at a distance until he had mastered it. Certainly he assigned the machine a minor role in his architecture.

Engineering was also subordinate in his work. He had an enormous ease with **structure**. His buildings were delicately weighted and balanced, and the full bearing load and tension integrity of each member was brought into play without calling attention to its performance. He regarded the engineered house—which developed quickly after the war—as a new romanticism which was replacing what he called "the romanticism of functionalism."

The 1944 Bethlehem Baptist Church was Schindler's only church commission. It replaced a building that had been destroyed by fire on a busy street in a depressed Negro area. Schindler overcame the disadvantages of the site by an L-shaped plan which embraced a garden, and by using walls of receding courses of stucco on two street fronts. The colors were indicative of his interest in the total plan; a mulberry gray that deepened into rosy violets and deep plums for the interiors. The scheme was based, he said, upon the skin tones of the worshippers.

Most of Schindler's later houses were designed for hillside lots, and were magnificently tucked into the surrounding greenery. This was partly due to the preliminary sketch he drew directly on a surveyor's map. The preliminary design was to him the vital one; in a letter published in *Pencil Points,* October, 1944, he wrote that it was "the very crux of the architect's contribution, his main creative effort."

His postwar houses became increasingly subjective and more difficult to read from the exterior. The interiors were a result of a passionately patient struggle with space. His deepening insights into human nuances were reflected in nuances of form; the houses were a kind of intimate portraiture in structure. The in-sloping walls of the 1947 Kallis house grew out of the owner's need for a studio in which light entered at right angles to the roof. The scheme was repeated in other walls and served to trap light for the rooms on the street side of the down-sloping lot. A gallery, developed out of an interior hall, was lighted by two clerestories,

(Text continued on page 192.)

Kallis house and studio, Los Angeles, 1945. Set on a steep lot, both house and studio had in-sloping walls.

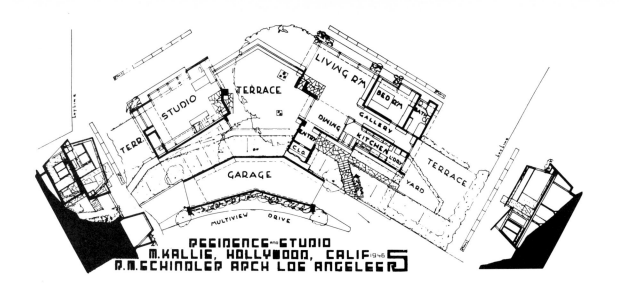

RESIDENCE and STUDIO
M. KALLIS, HOLLYWOOD, CALIF. 1946
R.M. SCHINDLER ARCH LOS ANGELES 5

View of the Kallis studio showing angle of the glass wall. The grooved 2 by 6-inch beams served as ceiling and surface for sheet roofing and formed wall sheathing.

The Kallis house living room, with deck visible through open door. Schindler often changed fenestration during construction; the large glass area at right was added when the house was half completed.

←

→

Kallis studio and deck as seen from the living room of the house. Openings were left in the deck for trees on the site.

Entrance, Daugherty house, Encino, 1946. Exterior plywood panels fastened to 2 by 4-inch stringers formed a fence along the covered entrance walk. The fence screened out the service yard.

→

Off the Daugherty house bedroom was a private balcony facing the hills to the north.

Above the stainless steel hood of the fireplace in the Lechner house was a trellis with philodendron. Triangular couches on either side faced the V-shaped hearth of Roman split brick in yellow earth tones.

The living room of the Lechner house, North Hollywood, 1948, faced a bowl-shaped canyon, around which rooms were arranged in an open U-shape. The dining chairs of plywood were designed by Schindler.

→

The Toole desert house, Palm Village, 1947, had stone-walled carport and entrance. Schindler looked upon the desert as savage and deliberately laid the stone to resemble leopard spots. Between the levels of the stepped roof were ventilating windows. The lowest roof was extended by a trellis to shade the porch on the east.

Schindler introduced corrugated plastic into the design of two houses built in 1949. Plastic formed a roofing material for part of the Tischler house (shown above). Canvas stretched on rings and fastened to the walls by tie-rods cut the glare before shade trees were established. The free-standing fireplace had a bent stainless steel hood. The low-cost Janson house (shown below), which grew like a light vine up a canyon side, used plastic for some of the walls; at night they were lighted from the exterior "to release color into the air."

and the upswept roof functioned as a reflector.

The wit in Schindler's houses often grew out of the site. The small 1942 Harris house seemed to be an extension of the granite block on which it was perched. The 1950 Janson house was a veritable jack-in-the-beanstalk structure; it grew like a light vine from the bottom of a canyon up to the road, clinging to the narrow ledge of level land at the top by structural tendrils.

Several times during his last years Schindler spoke of Gill's interrupted career. Gill's decline in popularity was like a cold wind that had blown too close to Schindler's own door. He once said that what he feared most was to end his life "puttering in architecture as Gill did." He recalled visiting Gill during the twenties when Gill lived on Ninth and Figueroa in Los Angeles, and said (his voice dropping almost to a whisper as if speaking of a tragedy), "I never once saw him at his drawing board."

But Schindler worked almost up to the time of his death. When he went to the hospital for an operation he wrote me, "I feel as if I had left an old house to enter a new room—small, circumscribed, with bare walls and only one exit." But a month later he was back at work. Although he was alone in the office, he was accomplishing as much work, he said, as when he had a draftsman.

At the end of the year he went again to the hospital for a second operation. One of his former draftsmen, Vick Santocchi, came back into the office, and took drawings to the hospital each morning for Schindler to revise.

In the hospital, by a curious coincidence, he shared a room with Richard Neutra for a week. Schindler had been an open critic of Neutra's work for a number of years but constant laughter issued from the room as they discussed their student days and the work of their contemporaries.

Schindler died of cancer on August 22, 1953.

At the opening of the Schindler memorial exhibition the gallery was packed. Scores of people waited for an hour or more on the street for a chance to see the first full showing of his work—the work of a man whom Talbot Hamlin, in a tribute written for the exhibition, called "the least understood and the least appreciated of the American pioneers of modern architecture."

Harris house, Los Angeles, 1942. Built of studs and plaster, it was an extension of the site—a small, steep shelf of decomposed granite.

ILLUSTRATION CREDITS

Key: t=top, b=bottom, l=left, r=right

INDEX